ELISHA

THE DOUBLE BLESSED PROPHET

DR. DAVID JEREMIAH

with Dr. David Jeremiah

P.O. Box 3838
San Diego, CA 92163

Edited by William Kruidenier
Unless otherwise indicated, Scripture verses quoted are taken from the NEW KING JAMES VERSION.

Printed in the United States of America.

CONTENTS

About Dr. David Jeremiah and Turning Point

Dr. David Jeremiah is the founder of Turning Point, a ministry committed to providing Christians with sound Bible teaching relevant to today's changing times through radio and television broadcasts, audio series, books, and live events. Dr. Jeremiah's common-sense teaching on topics such as family, prayer, worship, angels, and biblical prophecy forms the foundation of Turning Point.

David and his wife, Donna, reside in El Cajon, California, where he serves as the senior pastor of Shadow Mountain Community Church. David and Donna have four children and twelve grandchildren.

In 1982, Dr. Jeremiah brought the same solid teaching to San Diego television that he shares weekly with his congregation. Shortly thereafter, Turning Point expanded its ministry to radio. Dr. Jeremiah's inspiring messages can now be heard worldwide on radio, television, and the Internet.

Because Dr. Jeremiah desires to know his listening audience, he travels nationwide holding ministry rallies and events that touch the hearts and lives of many people. According to Dr. Jeremiah, "At some point in time, everyone reaches a turning point; and for every person, that moment is unique, an experience to hold onto forever. There's so much changing in today's world that sometimes it's difficult to choose the right path. Turning Point offers people an understanding of God's Word as well as the opportunity to make a difference in their lives."

Dr. Jeremiah has authored numerous books, including ***Escape the Coming Night*** (Revelation), ***The Handwriting on the Wall*** (Daniel), ***Overcoming Loneliness, Prayer—The Great Adventure, Captured by Grace, Signs of Life, Agents of the Apocalypse, Agents of Babylon, A Life Beyond Amazing, Forward, Everything You Need, Shelter in God, The Jesus You May Not Know,*** and ***The God You May Not Know***.

How to Use This Study Guide

The purpose of this Turning Point study guide is to reinforce Dr. David Jeremiah's dynamic, in-depth teaching and to aid the reader in applying biblical truth to his or her daily life. This study guide is designed to be used in conjunction with Dr. Jeremiah's *Elisha: The Double Blessed Prophet* audio series, but it may also be used by itself for personal or group study.

Structure of the Lessons

Each lesson is based on one of the messages in the *Elisha: The Double Blessed Prophet* compact disc series and focuses on specific passages in the Bible. Each lesson is composed of the following elements:

- *Outline*

The outline at the beginning of the lesson gives a clear, concise picture of the topic being studied and provides a helpful framework for readers as they listen to Dr. Jeremiah's teaching.

- *Overview*

The overview summarizes Dr. Jeremiah's teaching on the passage being studied in the lesson. Readers should refer to the Scripture passages in their own Bibles as they study the overview. Unless otherwise indicated, Scripture verses quoted are taken from the New King James Version.

- *Personal and Group Application Questions*

This section contains a variety of questions designed to help readers dig deeper into the lesson and the Scriptures, and to apply the lesson to their daily lives. For Bible study groups or Sunday school classes, these questions will provide a springboard for group discussion and interaction.

- *Did You Know?*

This section presents a fascinating fact, historical note, or insight that adds a point of interest to the preceding lesson.

Personal Study

Thank you for selecting *Elisha: The Double Blessed Prophet* for your current study. The lessons in this study guide were created to help you gain fresh insights into God's Word and develop new perspectives on topics you may have previously studied. Each lesson is designed to challenge your thinking, and help you grow in your knowledge of Christ. During your study, it is our prayer that you will discover how biblical truth affects every aspect of your life and your relationship with Christ will be strengthened.

When you commit to completing this study guide, try to set apart a time, daily or weekly, to read through the lessons without distraction. Have your Bible nearby when you read the study guide, so you're ready to look up verses if you need to. If you want to use a notebook to write down your thoughts, be sure to have that handy as well. Take your time to think through and answer the questions. If you plan on reading the study guide with a small group, be sure to read ahead and be prepared to take part in the weekly discussions.

Leader's Guide

Thank you for your commitment to lead a group through *Elisha: The Double Blessed Prophet*. Being a leader has its own rewards. You may discover that your walk with the Lord deepens through this experience. Throughout the study guide, your group will explore new topics and review study questions that encourage thought-provoking group discussion.

The lessons in this study guide are suitable for Sunday school classes, small-group studies, elective Bible studies, or home Bible study groups. Each lesson is structured to provoke thought and help you grow in your knowledge and understanding of God. There are multiple components in this section that can help you structure your lessons and discussion time, so make sure you read and consider each one.

Before You Begin

Before you begin each meeting, make sure you and your group are well-versed with the content of the chapter. Every person should have his or her own study guide so they can follow along and write in the study guide if need be. When possible, the study guide should be used with the corresponding compact disc series. You may wish to assign the study guide lesson as homework prior to the meeting of the group and then use the meeting time to listen to the CD and discuss the lesson.

To ensure that everyone has a chance to participate in the discussion, the ideal size for a group is around eight to ten people. If there are more than ten people, try to break up the bigger group into smaller subgroups. Make sure the members are committed to participating each week, as this will help create stability and help you better prepare the structure of the meeting.

At the beginning of the study each week, start the session with a question to challenge group members to think about the issues you will be discussing. The members can answer briefly, but the goal is to have an idea in their mind as you go over the lesson. This allows the group members to become engaged and ready to interact with the group.

After reviewing the lesson, try to initiate a free-flowing discussion. Invite group members to bring questions and insights they may have discovered to the next meeting, especially if they were unsure of the meaning of some parts of the lesson. Be prepared to discuss how biblical truth applies to the world we live in today.

Weekly Preparation

As the group leader, here are a few things you can do to prepare for each meeting:

- Choose whether or not you will play the CD message during your small group session.

  If you decide to play the CD message from Dr. Jeremiah as part of the meeting, you will need to adjust the group time accordingly.

- Make sure you are thoroughly familiar with the material in the lesson.

  Make sure you understand the content of the lesson so you know how to structure group time and you are prepared to lead group discussion.

- Decide, ahead of time, which questions you plan to discuss.

  Depending on how much time you have each week, you may not be able to reflect on every question. Select specific questions which you feel will evoke the best discussion.

- Take prayer requests.

  At the end of your discussion, take prayer requests from your group members and pray for each other.

Structuring the Discussion Time

If you need help in organizing your time when planning your group Bible study, here are two schedules, for sixty minutes and ninety minutes, which can give you a structure for the lesson:

Option 1 (Listen to Audio CD)	60 Minutes	90 Minutes
Welcome: Members arrive and get settled.	N/A	5 minutes
Getting Started Question: Prepares the group for interacting with one another.	Welcome and Getting Started 5 minutes	15 minutes
Message: Listen to the audio CD.	40 minutes	40 minutes
Discussion: Discuss group study questions.	10 minutes	25 minutes
Prayer and Application: Final application for the week and prayer before dismissal.	5 minutes	5 minutes

Option 2 (No Audio CD)	60 Minutes	90 Minutes
Welcome: Members arrive and get settled.	5 minutes	10 minutes
Getting Started Question: Prepares the group for interacting with one another.	10 minutes	10 minutes
Message: Review the lesson.	15 minutes	25 minutes
Discussion: Discuss group study questions.	25 minutes	35 minutes
Prayer and Application: Final application for the week and prayer before dismissal.	5 minutes	10 minutes

As the group leader, it is up to you to keep track of the time and keep things moving along according to your schedule. If your group is having a good discussion, don't feel the need to stop and move on to the next question. Remember, the purpose is to pull together ideas, and share unique insights on the lesson. Make time each week to discuss how to apply these truths to living for Christ today.

The purpose of discussion is for everyone to participate, but don't be concerned if certain group members are more quiet—they may be internally reflecting on the questions and need time to process their ideas before they can share them.

Group Dynamics

Leading a group study can be a rewarding experience for you and your group members—but that doesn't mean there won't be challenges. Certain members may feel uncomfortable discussing topics that they consider very personal, and might be afraid of being called on. Some members might have disagreements on specific issues. To help prevent these scenarios, consider the following ground rules:

- If someone has a question that may seem off topic, suggest that it is discussed at another time, or ask the group if they are okay with addressing that topic.
- If someone asks a question you don't know the answer to, confess that you don't know and move on. If you feel comfortable, invite other group members to give their opinions, or share their comments based on personal experience.
- If you feel like a couple of people are talking much more than others, direct questions to people who may not have shared yet. You could even ask the more dominating members to help draw out the quiet ones.
- When there is a disagreement, encourage the group members to process the matter in love. Invite members from opposing sides to evaluate their opinions and consider the ideas of the other members. Lead the group through Scripture that addresses the topic, and look for common ground.

When issues arise, remind your group to think of Scripture: "Love one another" (John 13:34), "If it is possible, as much as depends on you, live peaceably with all men" (Romans 12:18), and "Be quick to listen, slow to speak and slow to become angry" (James 1:19, NIV).

For Continuing Study

For a complete listing of Dr. Jeremiah's materials for personal and group study call 1-800-947-1993, go online to www.DavidJeremiah.org, or write to Turning Point, P.O. Box 3838, San Diego, CA 92163.

Dr. Jeremiah's *Turning Point* program is currently heard or viewed around the world on radio, television, and the Internet in English. *Momento Decisivo*, the Spanish translation of Dr. Jeremiah's messages, can be heard on radio in every Spanish speaking country in the world. The television broadcast is also broadcast by satellite throughout the Middle East with Arabic subtitles.

Contact Turning Point for radio and television program times and stations in your area, or visit our website at www.DavidJeremiah.org/stationlocator.

ELISHA:
THE DOUBLE BLESSED PROPHET

INTRODUCTION

See if you can find the common thread running through these pairs of well-known people: Steve Jobs and Mark Zuckerberg. Dr. Benjamin Mays and Dr. Martin Luther King, Jr. Woody Guthrie and Bob Dylan. Father Michael van der Peet and Mother Teresa. Pope John Paul II and Pope Benedict XVI. Warren Buffett and Bill Gates. Ray Charles and Quincy Jones. Ralph Waldo Emerson and Henry David Thoreau. Obi-Wan Kenobi and Luke Skywalker. Socrates and Plato.

And on a more familiar plane, consider these: Moses and Joshua. Paul and Timothy. Barnabas and John Mark. Jesus and Peter, James, and John.

In each pair of names, the first person was a mentor to the second. Or, said another way, the second person was a protégé of the first. To varying degrees and in different ways, these mentors greatly influenced the life and development of their mentees.

As the varied names illustrate, mentor/mentee relationships are not culture or career specific. They can be found throughout history at every strata of society. They are how learning, values, traditions, skills, and encouragement are passed from one generation to the next. Every parent is called to be a mentor, and most successful people can point to someone who was an influence in their life.

When it comes to biblical history, Moses and Joshua might get the nod as the best-known mentor/protégé pair in the Old Testament. But close on their heels—and top of the list among the prophets—was the relationship between the mentor, Elijah, and his protégé, Elisha.

This Turning Point study guide, *Elisha: The Double Blessed Prophet,* is about the younger of the Elijah/Elisha pair. It is not about their relationship, but in the first lesson, "Burning Your Bridges," you will discover insights into who Elisha was against the backdrop of his mentor's larger-than-life, sometimes-up and sometimes-down life and ministry. Elijah was a power-prophet, always representing God on big stages, winning big battles.

Elisha, on the other hand, was a people-prophet. To be sure, Elisha interfaced with kings at times, but he was characterized more by compassion than by conquest. While Elijah was the prophet of the extraordinary, Elisha was the prophet of the ordinary—ordinary in the sense of meeting the same needs in peoples' lives that you and I might have some three thousand years later. God used them both in miraculous ways, but their miracles tended to trend in different directions.

For the last decade of Elijah's ministry, Elisha shadowed him. At God's direction, Elijah anointed Elisha—a young farmer from a prosperous family—to be his successor. Elisha left home—burned his bridges, we might say—and devoted his life to his teacher and mentor. When it came time for Elijah to depart, Elisha had seen his mentor represent God with courage and confidence, and sometimes cowardice. Elisha took the training and life lessons he learned from Elijah and incorporated it all into his own ministry that lasted half a century in Israel, after which he died at nearly ninety years of age.

This study guide doesn't cover all of Elisha's miracles—the Old Testament records twice as many miracles of Elisha as of Elijah. But we will explore a variety of them that expose the heart of a prophet who committed himself to serving God above all else. No other person in the Bible worked the variety of miracles that Elisha did. No need was too large—like defeating an invading army—or too small—like restoring a lost tool to a worker—for Elisha to consider.

Most importantly, Elisha's heart represented the heart of God; a prophet's ultimate mentor is God Himself. We learn from Elisha that no need in the lives of God's people is too large or too small for His compassionate attention—even needs that require a miracle.

Burning Your Bridges

1 Kings 19:19-21

In this lesson we are introduced to Elisha, the protégé of the prophet Elijah.

OUTLINE

The Christian life is a series of decisions, the first one being the decision to trust in Jesus Christ as Lord and Savior. But then comes a lifetime of decisions to follow God's will and God's call in our life as we discover more of His plan. Elisha is a model of how to say "Yes" to God.

I. **Elisha's Character**
   A. He Was Compassionate
   B. He Was Courageous
   C. He Was Consistent
   D. He Was Christlike

II. **Elisha's Call**
   A. Elisha Responded Immediately
   B. Elisha Responded Thoughtfully
   C. Elisha Responded Decisively

Are you familiar with a writer named Sherwood Anderson? If not, don't feel bad; most people are not. But how about these writers: Ernest Hemingway, William Faulkner, Thomas Wolfe, and John Steinbeck? Most readers know the names of these last four. But what they likely don't know is what the four had in common. They were all mentored, as young and aspiring writers, by Sherwood Anderson.

It's often the case that the mentor stands in the shadow of his or her protégé(s). And that is very nearly the case with two of the Old Testament's most famous prophets: Elijah, the mentor, and Elisha, the protégé. As we will discover, Elisha received a double portion of Elijah's gifting and performed twice as many miracles as his mentor. Though they are both well known, Elisha learned well from Elijah, his mentor in the prophetic office.

In this study guide, we will delve into the life and times of Elisha. First, we'll discover how God used this prophet to speak to the nation of Israel. Second, we'll look for spiritual lessons to be drawn from Elisha's life to apply to our lives today.

Elisha's Character

Elisha was born in the ninth century B.C., the son of a well-to-do farmer in the Jordan Valley south of the Sea of Galilee. He soon emerged as the leader of the prophets in that area as they defended their ministry from the evil king and queen of the ten northern tribes of Israel, Ahab and Jezebel.

He Was Compassionate

Some miracles in the Old Testament were used as a form of judgment, but almost all of Elisha's miracles were motivated by compassion. For instance, he purified a polluted spring in Jericho; he provided financial resources for a widow; he asked God to give a barren woman a son, then raised the son back to life years later; he multiplied food stores to alleviate a famine; he healed a powerful military commander of leprosy.

Elijah's miracles were statements of power or authority. Elisha's miracles were statements of compassion and help.

He Was Courageous

But Elisha was no shrinking violet; he was no coward. He wasn't afraid to speak truth to power. On one occasion, the king of Aram sent a huge army with horses and chariots to capture Elisha. To calm his frightened servant, Elisha asked the Lord to open the servant's eyes so he could see the chariots of fire (belonging to God) filling the hillsides around them. Then Elisha asked the Lord to strike the advancing army of Aram with blindness (and then asked that their sight be restored). Elisha was no coward; he called on God for deliverance when needed (2 Kings 6:8-18).

Another time, Elisha refused a gift from a commander named Naaman, whom Elisha had healed. God had told him not to take the gift—at the risk of insulting a powerful man. But Elisha stood his ground, preferring to insult the commander rather than disobey God (2 Kings 5:16).

The following words on courage are attributed to the late Rev. Billy Graham: "Courage is contagious. When a brave man takes a stand, the spines of those around him are stiffened." Elisha was a man, a prophet, who strengthened the spines of the young prophets who gathered around him.

He Was Consistent

Not only was Elisha compassionate and courageous, he was consistent. Elijah had been impulsive, emotional; he could turn on a dime. He could defeat the prophets of Baal one minute then flee for his life from Jezebel the next. But Elisha wasn't like his mentor. He was steady and consistent in his personality and prophetic ministry. God used Elijah, just as He used the sometimes-impulsive Peter in the New Testament. But impulsiveness didn't characterize Elisha; he showed up on time, every time, as the saying goes.

He Was Christlike

Compassion, courage, consistency—who does that remind you of? In those ways, and others, Elisha was like Jesus Christ. Many things in Elisha's life were typical of the Christ who would come centuries later.

- Their names: Elisha means "God is salvation"; Jesus (Hebrew Joshua) means "Jehovah is salvation."
- Their ministries: Both started their ministries at the Jordan River. Elisha took up Elijah's mantle there; Jesus was baptized there.

- Their ministry to widows: Both Elisha and Jesus raised the dead sons of widows back to life—Elisha, the son of a Shunammite widow; Jesus, the son of a widow of Nain.
- Their miracles of feeding: Elisha fed a hundred men with a few loaves, and Christ fed thousands on two occasions with a few loaves and fish.
- Their miracles of multiplication: Elisha multiplied a small amount of oil into enough for a community, and Jesus turned water into wine at a wedding.
- Their miracles of healing leprosy: Elisha cured the leprosy of Naaman, and Jesus healed numerous lepers.
- Their miracles of physics: Elisha made an iron ax float on water, and Jesus walked on water (and enabled Peter to do the same), defying the laws of physics.
- Their betrayal for money: Elisha was betrayed for money by his servant Gehazi, and Jesus was betrayed for money by His disciple Judas.[1]

In many ways, Elisha foreshadowed the ministry of Jesus Christ in the New Testament. Elisha is one more way that the Old Testament points forward to the Bible's central character, Jesus.

Elisha's Call

Elisha first appears on the scene in 1 Kings 19 as he answers a call from God. His response is a pattern we would do well to follow.

Elisha Responded Immediately

God told Elijah that Elisha was to be his successor (1 Kings 19:16). Elijah had been through a difficult time following the confrontation with the prophets of Baal on Mount Carmel, after which he fled to Mount Horeb to hide. It was there that God told him to seek out Elisha and anoint him as his (Elijah's) successor. Elijah found Elisha plowing a field and threw his mantle (cloak) on his shoulders, a sign that Elisha would inherit Elijah's ministry.

Elisha's response to Elijah was immediate: "And [Elisha] left the oxen and ran after Elijah" (1 Kings 19:20). That is the response servants of God should have. Even if our calling is not as clear and objective as Elisha's, we should live with a sense of immediacy about following God's call, whatever we think it may be. Elisha didn't want to miss out and neither should we.

Whenever you sense God's call—through reading Scripture, through prayer, through godly counsel—respond immediately. If you delay, you give the enemy of your soul an opportunity to convince you not to follow. Don't wait; follow God like Elisha did —immediately. Don't postpone until tomorrow something God wants you to do today. We are not promised tomorrow, so don't presume it will come.

Elisha Responded Thoughtfully

Elisha responded immediately but not impulsively (1 Kings 19:20). He surely had many thoughts racing through his mind about what this call meant. His first thought was to seek out his parents to say goodbye. Elijah affirmed that request as if to say, "Don't rush; count the cost; honor your parents." This action of Elisha was consistent with his steady character—decisive but not impulsive, consistent but not careless. Putting his parents before himself was a sign of his character.

Elisha Responded Decisively

Elisha's decisiveness is the key part of his calling. Elisha took one of the pairs of oxen and slaughtered them, building a fire from the yoke and harness, and cooked the meat. There were likely several reasons for this. Killing his oxen was a way to burn the bridges leading back to his old way of life. He was now a prophet and there was no going back. It was also a cause for celebration as he shared the food with others in a feast to honor God's call on his life.

Elisha told himself and his community that he was leaving to begin a new adventure with God. It was the most decisive moment in his life! When God speaks to us and sets us on a new path, we need to respond the same way—with determination and decisiveness regarding our new direction. By killing his oxen, the means of his livelihood, he was removing the temptation to return and take up farming again.

Erwin McManus has written, "One of the inescapable themes of the Scripture is that we cannot grab hold of the future if we keep holding onto the past."[2] People today will say, "I want to keep my options open; I don't want to close any doors. I want to have something to fall back on in case this other thing doesn't work out." Not Elisha! He didn't want options; he only wanted the will of God for his life. He closed all other doors and walked through the open door God showed him.

In further lessons in this study guide, we'll see all these characteristics of Elisha demonstrated: compassion, courage, consistency, and Christlikeness. We'll find him acting surely, deliberately, and decisively. His ministry began with the singular action of closing all doors except the one God showed him. He got rid of all options except the option of obedience. He entertained only one purpose—to fulfill the call of God on his life.

Jesus had the same perspective and He communicated it to His followers: "If anyone comes to Me and does not hate his father and mother, wife and children, brothers and sisters, yes, and his own life also, he cannot be My disciple. And whoever does not bear his cross and come after Me cannot be My disciple" (Luke 14:26-27). Jesus did not mean we should hate our parents; He meant we should do like Elisha did: honor them, but do not put them in a higher place than God in our life. This is a hard saying—especially the part about taking up our cross, that is, being willing to die for Christ—and yet such a decision is required of all who would follow God.

It is threatening to consider "hating" one's life. But Jesus meant that we must be willing to change our life's course if that is what God indicates we are to do. We like the comfort of our routines in life; we do not get up every day wishing for change and disruption. We know how the day is going to begin and end—and then God calls us to do something different. It's challenging! But we must consider it and be prepared for it. Our call may not come as suddenly as Elisha's did, which is in our favor. We have time to consider the cost of following Christ and prepare ourselves for the possibility of change.

It's another way of looking at the Christian life. Paul says our citizenship is in heaven though we dwell on earth (Philippians 3:20). Our mindset must be the mindset of heaven. We cannot live with one spiritual and emotional foot on earth and the other in heaven. We have to live with the mindset of immediacy, thoughtfulness, and decisiveness, all in anticipation of God's call on our life.

It comes down to what Elisha did; it comes down to decisions. The first big decision is to choose to receive God's gift of forgiveness and eternal life through faith in Christ. Then, the Christian life is a daily decision to be obedient to God's call and path. Since that call may not come in as clear a way as it did for Elisha, we listen for indicators and leadings as we live out the disciple's life of following Christ. Our spiritual ears are constantly attuned to what God may be speaking to us. We live in a continual state of readiness to hear and do the will of God.

Do you know the words of the classic hymn, "I Have Decided to Follow Jesus"? Many lyrics from that hymn are well-known to churchgoers: "Though none go with me, I still will follow"; "The world behind me, the cross before me"; and the chorus, "No turning back, no turning back." Is that not a beautiful portrayal of Elisha's response to follow God's call?

But that's not all; there is a tradition behind the words of that hymn. In 1904-1905, a great revival swept through Wales, known today as the Welsh Revival, resulting in many conversions. Missionary activity was born out of the revival, and one Welsh man traveled to India to spread the Gospel. He ventured into a mountainous region, heading for a remote village known for its violent ways. He was warned not to go there but travelled on.

He arrived and was able to win one native man and his family to Christ. That family decided they must share the Good News with others in their tribe. But the chief was angry and threatened them. Before the whole tribe the chief demanded they stop following Jesus.

The tribesman replied, "No. I have decided to follow Jesus. I am not turning back." So the chief killed the tribesman's children and threatened the man again. But he replied, "Though no one joins me, still I will follow."

So the chief killed the tribesman's wife, demanding again that he stop following Jesus. The tribesman looked the chief in the eyes and replied, "The cross before me, the world behind me, no turning back!" So the chief killed the tribesman.

Like the grain of wheat that falls into the ground and dies, new life was the result of those deaths (John 12:24). After witnessing the steadfastness of the tribesman and his family, many members of the tribe decided to follow Jesus as well. Even the chief became a follower of Christ. The tribesman's words became a song the tribe sang in honor of the tribesman who showed them how to live and die for Christ—a song that became the hymn "I Have Decided to Follow Jesus" years later.[3]

Have you decided to follow Jesus? Perhaps you have decided to follow Him as your Savior and your pathway to eternal life. But are you prepared to follow Him wherever that path may lead while you are still on earth? Let Elisha be a challenge to you as you complete this study guide. Let His faithfulness as a prophet of God —never an easy calling—motivate you to evaluate your own readiness and willingness to burn your bridges each time God makes His will clear to you.

Notes

1. Rev. Martine Oborne, "10 Similarities Between Jesus and the Prophet Elisha," November 27, 2018, https://www.martineoborne.com/10-similarities-between-jesus-and-the-prophet-elisha/.
2. Erwin Raphael McManus, *The Last Arrow* (New York, NY: Waterbrook Press 2017), 37-38.
3. "The True Story Behind the Song 'I Have Decided to Follow Jesus,'" *Renewal Journal*, accessed July 31, 2020.

PERSONAL QUESTIONS

1. When did you personally make a decision to follow Christ?

   a. Did you burn any bridges when you decided to follow Christ? Explain.

   b. As you have grown in Christ, what other bridges have you burned as you have deepened your walk with Him?

2. Write in one or two sentences what you believe God's call on your life is at this time.

a. How did you arrive at that understanding?

b. Do you remain confident in your calling? Do you sense God is calling you to something new? Explain.

c. Are there any "bridges" in your life you feel hesitant to "burn" as you follow Christ? How do you plan to resolve that conflict?

3. Read Luke 14:26-27.

a. How have Jesus' words been applied in your own family / friends' experience?

b. How does the idea of taking up your cross (dying for Christ) make you think about following Him?

c. What might be an example of "hating" family or friends when it comes to following Christ?

d. Describe any costly choices you've had to make as you have followed Christ.

4. Compare Jesus' words in Luke 9:62 with Elisha's "burning of his bridges" response. How does Elisha serve as an example of Jesus' words?

GROUP QUESTIONS

1. Share your understanding of God's calling on your life with the group.

   a. How did individual members discern God's calling?

   b. Have they sensed a change in God's calling over the years? How was it made known?

   c. What are the best ways to *discern* the call of God?

   d. What are the best ways to *confirm* the call of God?

2. Discuss Elisha's decision to follow Elijah with Jesus' response to several people in Luke 9:57-62, especially verses 61-62. (See 1 Kings 19:20)

   a. Why do you think Elisha's momentary delay was acceptable to Elijah compared to Jesus' response to a similar request? (verses 61-62)

b. How might the process of discerning God's call involve reasonable delays in today's complicated world?

c. How are small steps toward God's call evidence of an acceptance of His call?

3. Read Luke 14:28-35.

   a. What is the theme of this section of Jesus' teaching?

   b. How was Elisha able to "count the cost" of following Elijah so quickly, a decision that proved sure for the rest of his life?

   c. What happens to us if we "lose our saltiness"? (verse 34)

d. Were you, as a new Christian, encouraged to "count the cost" of following Christ? Would it have made an impact on you if you had been?

4. How would you counsel a friend or child as to discerning and affirming God's call on his or her life?

DID YOU KNOW?

When the greater preacher-evangelist, D. L. Moody, first started to preach the Gospel in Chicago, he would say at the end of each service, "I want you to go home tonight and think about what I've said and come back tomorrow night ready to make a decision for Christ." And for years that was his standard procedure. On Sunday, October 8, 1871, he dismissed the congregation with that exhortation. But that night, the Great Chicago Fire broke out and burned for three days. Some who perished were members of Moody's church; they never returned to the next service. Possibly some perished without making a decision to follow Christ. From that day until he died, Moody never again used that closing exhortation. He didn't want anyone to put off until tomorrow what needed to be done today.

The Double Blessing

1 Kings 19:21–2 Kings 2:15

In this lesson we discover how and why Elisha received a double blessing from God.

OUTLINE

Sometimes Christians are hesitant to ask God to bless them; it seems greedy or selfish. But Elisha did, along with others that God used. But the blessing Elisha received was more than just a blessing for himself. It was a blessing that equipped him to be a blessing to others.

I. The Relationship Behind the Double Blessing
- A. The Loyalty of Elisha
- B. The Love of Elisha

II. The Ritual Before the Double Blessing

III. The Request That Produced the Double Blessing

IV. The Response That Asked for the Double Blessing

V. The Requirement That Restricted the Double Blessing

VI. The Reaction That Validated the Double Blessing

VII. Conclusion
- A. God Wants You to Seek His Blessing
- B. Every Time God Blesses You It Is a Potential Double Blessing
- C. God's Blessing Comes With Responsibility

OVERVIEW

The Bible is a book about blessings; the Hebrew word for blessing occurs more than three hundred times in the Old Testament! The story of redemption is the story of God blessing mankind with the opportunity to reestablish a relationship with Him. This lesson is about a man who sought God's blessing and received it—a prophet named Elisha.

In the previous lesson, we learned that God told the prophet Elijah to anoint Elisha to be his successor. Elijah took off his mantle and put it on Elisha's shoulders, a symbolic way of passing the prophetic torch to the younger man. We also saw that Elisha accepted God's call and followed Elijah after bidding his family goodbye. He cut his ties with his family and his vocation as a farmer and held a feast for his community. He made a public declaration of his intent to follow God's will for his life. He humbled himself by becoming the protégé of his mentor, Elijah.

For the next ten years Elijah and Elisha ministered together; Elijah was decreasing in prominence and Elisha was increasing. Though he was Elijah's successor, for ten years Elisha humbly served the older prophet in ministry. We pick up the story of Elisha as he receives a double blessing from God.

The Relationship Behind the Double Blessing

Elisha's double blessing wasn't a random event. It was given as a result of the loyalty and love Elisha manifested toward Elijah.

The Loyalty of Elisha

The first thing we read about Elisha is that he "arose and followed Elijah, and became his servant" (1 Kings 19:21). During the time in which Elisha served Elijah, he was mentored and trained in prophetic ministry in preparation for Elijah's departure from earth.

When the time of Elijah's departure drew near, the two prophets were on a final ministry trip together (2 Kings 2). They were leaving Gilgal, headed for Bethel, when Elijah instructed Elisha to remain behind. This instruction for Elisha to remain behind happened three times—in verses 2, 4, and 6 in relation to Bethel, Jericho, and the Jordan River. Apparently, Elisha didn't heed this instruction because Elijah repeats it three times. We don't know exactly what was going on there; Elijah was beginning to distance himself from his young protégé for some reason.

What we do know is that Elisha, for his own reasons, refused to be left behind; he refused to be separated from his mentor, Elijah (2 Kings 2:2, 4, 6). Perhaps it was just pure loyalty that kept Elisha close to Elijah. Perhaps Elisha felt a need to stay with the older prophet for his protection. The Bible doesn't elaborate on this curious exchange between the two men.

The Love of Elisha

At Bethel, a group of prophets asked Elisha if he knew the Lord was preparing to take Elijah to heaven (2 Kings 2:3). Elisha knew, but told them not to speak of it. The same thing happened at Jericho (verse 5). Again, no explanation is given for Elisha's refusal to interact with the prophets about Elijah's impending departure. Perhaps Elijah's departure was weighing heavily on Elisha; perhaps it was a matter of grief to him that he simply didn't want to face up to or discuss with others. If so, his reluctance would be understandable.

Elijah and Elisha had ministered together for ten years, probably in each other's company daily. Elisha had witnessed many of the miracles that occurred through Elijah. What an emotional decade it must have been! And now there were indications that their relationship was soon to end. Maybe he was in some sort of denial, just not wanting to lose the companionship of his mentor. We can easily say that Elisha's love for Elijah was deep and genuine.

The Ritual Before the Double Blessing

As the two prophets approached the Jordan River, they were met by a company of fifty prophets (2 Kings 2:7-8). Rather than wading across the river, Elijah took his robe, rolled it up, and slapped the water with it—and the river parted to the right and left, reminiscent of Moses parting the Red Sea. Elijah and Elisha walked across the riverbed "on dry ground." There is a sense of ceremony in this event, reminiscent of other special relationships in the Bible: Moses and Joshua, David and Solomon, Paul and Timothy, John the Baptist and Jesus—the end of one man's ministry and the beginning of another's.

The Request That Produced the Double Blessing

As they reach the far bank of the Jordan, Elijah says to Elisha, "Ask! What may I do for you, before I am taken away from you?" (2 Kings 2:9) This is an open invitation for Elisha to ask for whatever he needs before Elijah departs. The Lord said the same thing to Solomon (1 Kings 3:5); Jonathan said the same thing to David (1 Samuel 20:4); and Jesus issued the same invitation to His disciples (John 15:7). In every case, it exhibited covenant love: "What I have is yours; just ask."

When Solomon gave his request to God, it was not for wealth or power, something a new, young king might be tempted to ask for. Instead, Solomon asked for wisdom to know how to lead and judge the nation of Israel with justice and righteousness. And God granted Solomon's request (1 Kings 3:12-13). It should come as no surprise that Solomon's wisdom became known far and wide. Solomon asked for wisdom and discernment, and God granted his request. But, because Solomon didn't ask for riches, God granted him "riches and honor" as well—and his kingdom became the wealthiest on earth. Solomon's priorities were in line with God's and he was rewarded for it.

The Response That Asked for the Double Blessing

Elisha's request to Elijah was similar to Solomon's in terms of priorities. Elisha didn't ask for fame or power; he simply asked for "a double portion" of Elijah's spirit to be upon him (2 Kings 2:9). Elisha had seen how God had used Elijah and he wanted to be used even more. Elisha's request calls to mind Jesus' promise to His disciples that they would do "greater works" than He had done when He departed (John 14:12).

Elisha probably looked upon himself as Elijah's "firstborn" prophetic son—in the Old Testament, the firstborn son had the right to a double portion of the father's inheritance. Rather than his request being viewed as arrogant or selfish, Elisha probably saw it as a matter of being honored as Elijah's protégé. And his request was granted: Elisha's ministry was twice the length of Elijah's and witnessed twice as many miracles.

It's all in the request. God is happy to grant requests that are in His will, and what Elisha asked for was in God's will. That remains a governing principle of prayer to this day (James 4:3). Elijah was leaving, but God was staying with Elisha because Elisha's heart was turned toward God with pure purposes.

The Requirement That Restricted the Double Blessing

Elisha's request was granted—on one condition. Prophets were intense, sometimes complicated, people. And here Elijah introduces a variable, the purpose of which is not immediately clear: In order for Elisha to inherit a double portion of Elijah's spirit, Elisha would have to witness Elijah's departure into heaven. And that happened: Elisha witnessed Elijah going up into the heavens in a chariot of fire and a whirlwind (2 Kings 2:10-12).

What was the point of that condition? Again, it is not totally clear. R. T. Kendall's view on this matter is worth considering. He notes that Elijah said that Elisha's request was "a hard thing" (2 Kings 2:10). Not hard for God, surely. So it must have been hard for Elijah—hard to agree to his protégé superseding him in ministry. But he agreed, on the condition that Elisha be with him when he departed—that is, that Elisha not abandon him.

Kendall observes wryly, "I can safely tell you that Elisha was in Elijah's face from that moment, being careful not to look up, down or sideways—not even daring to sneeze."[1] Elisha wasn't going to take his eyes off of Elijah! He wanted the blessing of God on his ministry.

And so it happened. After a decade of being together every day, Elijah was taken to heaven and Elisha was on his own.

The Reaction That Validated the Double Blessing

Did the transfer of ministry from Elijah to Elisha actually happen? Nothing had happened yet to prove that it did—until Elisha's first act validated the transfer of blessing.

Elijah's mantle lay on the ground where it fell when he departed. Elisha picked it up and returned to the banks of the Jordan River. Doing what he had seen his mentor do, he struck the water with the mantle, and the river divided just as it had done when they first crossed over (2 Kings 2:13-14). When the company of prophets from Jericho saw this happen, they said, "The spirit of Elijah rests on Elisha" (verse 15). And they bowed down before him.

The company of prophets witnessed the transfer of office and power from Elijah to Elisha. The parting of the waters was God's validation that Elisha had succeeded Elijah. In the lessons ahead, we will see repeated validations of that transfer. We will see how the power of God flowed uninterrupted through Elisha the prophet.

What can we learn at this point in Elisha's story? How can we transfer spiritual lessons from his life to ours?

Conclusion

There are three lessons we can take away from this part of Elisha's story.

God Wants You to Seek His Blessing

Sometimes we forget: God wants us to seek His blessing. Solomon and Elisha asked for God's blessing and so did Jacob. When Jacob was returning to his homeland after trying to make things right with his brother, Esau, he encountered God (Genesis 32). In that encounter, Jacob told God, "I will not let You go unless You bless me!" (verse 26)

Mark Batterson offers this reflection on Jacob's words: "Jacob valued the blessing above all else. He wasn't just willing to fight for it. I think he was willing to die for it... The blessing of God is a gift from God. You cannot earn it, per se. But are you willing to risk life and limb for it? Are you willing to pull an all-nighter for it? Are you willing to go to the mat and get back up for it? With all of his faults, Jacob accurately estimated the value of the blessing!"[2]

Jacob wasn't going to let go of God until God blessed him. And he received the blessing. I know of no place in Scripture where someone is told *not* to ask for God's blessing or is rebuked for asking. I conclude that it is acceptable for us to ask for God's blessing. The problem is we don't feel right in asking for God's blessing; we feel like it is somehow wrong.

I felt that way when I was a young pastor starting a church in Indiana. Our first Sunday we had 35 people in attendance. I did everything I could to learn how to grow the church—except ask God to bless the teaching of His Word and to bless us for wanting to grow His Kingdom. I traveled to conferences where I listened to megachurch pastors and wondered if I would ever be able to have their kind of impact. I lived with the idea that it was wrong to ask God to bless me, thinking if He wanted to bless me, He would do it in His own time and way.

I don't think that way anymore, and I hope you don't either. I know now that God wants to bless us, and it is not wrong to ask as long as we are asking for reasons that honor Him.

Every Time God Blesses You It Is a Potential Double Blessing

Elijah was blessed, but he turned his blessing into a blessing for others. His double blessing was not for him personally; it was for those whom he would minister to with the blessing of God. It's the same when God blesses us. The first blessing is when we are blessed, and the second blessing is when we bless others with that blessing.

The apostle Paul taught something from Jesus not recorded in the four Gospel accounts: "And remember the words of the Lord Jesus, that He said, 'It is more blessed to give than to receive'" (Acts 20:35). There are many beatitudes in the Bible ("blessed is," "blessed are"), but this is the only one that says "it is *more* blessed" —like a double blessing. It is more blessed to give than to receive.

Receiving from God is a blessing, but there is another blessing when we use what God has blessed us with to bless others. There's nothing wrong at all with receiving. We could never have any way to bless others without first receiving a blessing from God. When we give, we are imitating God. He gives to us, we give to others, they give to others, and on and on the cycle of blessing continues. The first blessing is when we receive, but the second blessing is when we give.

God's Blessing Comes With Responsibility

Jesus said that "to whom much is given, from him much will be required" (Luke 12:48). Every blessing becomes a matter of stewardship. Everything we have comes from God (1 Chronicles 29:14), so everything we have is a blessing from God. So then, every blessing from God becomes a matter of stewardship responsibility.

Sometimes God blesses us so richly that we don't feel we know how to manage, or steward, His blessing. For example, God blesses your church, your ministry, your business, or your family—and those blessings bring new responsibilities you hadn't imagined. But those responsibilities become additional reasons for God to bless our capacity and our capabilities for His glory.

When God blessed Elisha, his ministry exploded, and his life changed dramatically. He no doubt had moments in which he wondered if he could handle any more of God's "blessings" in his life. But God used Elisha's blessings to grow him into a more mature prophet and servant of God. And He will do the same for us if we will receive His blessing and the responsibilities that come with it.

Consider applying these three lessons to your life: Seek God's blessing in every area of your life that will bring glory to Him. But seek those blessings with the anticipation of blessing others. And seek them knowing they come with the responsibilities of stewardship. In doing so, you'll be following in the footsteps of the prophet Elisha—the doubly-blessed prophet of God.

Notes

1. R. T. Kendall, *These Are the Days of Elijah: How God Uses Ordinary People to Do Extraordinary Things* (Minneapolis, MN: Baker Publishing, 2013), 179.
2. Mark Batterson, *Double Blessing: How to Get It. How to Give It* (Sisters, OR: Multnomah Press, 2019), 66.

PERSONAL QUESTIONS

1. Read Deuteronomy 21:15-17.

   a. What provision is made in the law for the firstborn son?

   b. In what sense might Elisha have considered himself the firstborn of Elijah?

   c. As the *only* Son of His Father, what did Jesus receive? (Psalm 2:6-12)

   d. How might the double-portion law inform your understanding of the parable of the prodigal son and his older brother in Luke 15:28-31?

2. Read 1 Chronicles 4:9-10.

   a. What kind of blessing did Jabez ask of God?

   b. Given that God granted Jabez's request, what does that suggest about God's willingness to answer prayers for blessing?

c. Do you feel selfish or greedy when you pray for God's blessing? Why do you? Why should you not?

3. If we have inherited blessing from God, what should we share with others, even when we are not blessed by them? (1 Peter 3:8-9)

4. How did Jonathan demonstrate covenant loyalty (like Elijah in 2 Kings 2:9) to David? (1 Samuel 20:4)

a. How did Jesus demonstrate it to His disciples before His departure? (John 15:7)

b. How do you demonstrate loyalty to those around you? How should you?

c. Such relationships are rare (Proverbs 18:24). How many "covenant-level" friends do you have (like Elijah/Elisha or David/Jonathan)?

GROUP QUESTIONS

1. How do you feel about asking God to bless you or aspects of your life?

   a. Give some examples of requests for blessing you have made.

   b. How do you feel about the stewardship responsibility of your blessings?

   c. How does the concept of tithing fit into this discussion—blessing others with God's financial blessings?

2. Read Luke 11:9-13 together.

   a. How do verses 9-10 encourage us to ask God for blessings? Do these verses apply just to material needs or to any kind of blessing?

   b. How does your experience as a parent influence your understanding of verses 11-13?

   c. What do Jesus' words indicate about God's willingness to bless us?

   d. How willing are you to bless your own children? How much more willing is God to bless His children?

3. Are there areas of your life that you wish God would bless more richly?

    a. Have you asked Him for those blessings?

    b. What responsibilities might come with those blessings?

4. Consider Matthew 5:3-11. How many categories of blessing does Jesus list? Could His list be considered an invitation to seek those blessings (except for verses 10-11)?

5. Have a time of prayer where group members pray for God's blessings in areas that have been mentioned.

DID YOU KNOW?

Paul's quote of Jesus' words in Acts 20:35 follows a formula that came to be used in the Early Church: "Remember the words of the Lord Jesus, that He said . . . ." The same formula is found in another (non-canonical) writing from the first century, the First Epistle of Clement, attributed to Clement, the bishop of Rome. In his letter to the church at Corinth, Clement writes, "Remember the words of our Lord Jesus, for He said . . . ." (1 Clement 46:8). Clement quotes a saying of Jesus found in the Gospels, whereas Paul's quotation of Jesus is not found in the Gospels. However, this fact supports John 21:25 where the apostle says that a complete record of all Jesus' works would fill countless books. There was no doubt many things Jesus said—like the quote in Acts 20:35—were not recorded in any of the four Gospels.

THE ANATOMY OF A MIRACLE

2 Kings 4:1-7

In this lesson we follow the events that led to a miracle for a widow in need.

OUTLINE

Many of the miracles of Elisha parallel the miracles of Jesus Christ—acts of compassion in response to a desperate human need. These miracles were often the result of an interaction between the one in need and the miracle worker—combining need, cooperation, and faith.

I. The Cry
- A. Death
- B. Debt
- C. Destitution

II. The Command

III. The Commitment

IV. The Conclusion
- A. The Principle of Personal Desperation
- B. The Principle of Divine Cooperation
- C. The Principle of Potential Limitation

OVERVIEW

There are more miracles in the life of Elisha than we can cover in this one series of lessons, so we will focus on the ones from which we can draw the best applications for the Christian life today. There are four miracles in 2 Kings 4 alone! And we will look at the first of those in this lesson: the miracle of the widow's oil. It is a miracle in which God meets the needs of a desperate individual, something we can all identify with at times.

THE CRY

In 2 Kings 4:1-2, a widow of one of the prophets cries out to Elisha for help. She is desperate for three reasons.

Death

The woman's husband was one of the company of prophets who served under Elisha, but her husband had died, leaving her with nothing. Her husband had been a godly man, by his widow's own testimony, a man who "feared the Lord" (verse 1).

As often as Jesus made allusions to the Old Testament, one wonders if He had this story of the widow in mind in His own story of a widow and an unjust judge (Luke 18:1-5). In that story, a widow cried out for justice (for help) to an unjust judge who finally relented "because this widow troubles me [with her persistent requests]." The widow basically wore the judge out with her persistent pleading.

There is no explicit indication that the widow who came to Elisha did that, but the two widows' situations are similar: desperate needs which they brought unashamedly to an authority they thought could help. The widow in Elisha's situation was in trouble, and she wasn't afraid to ask for help. But there was a specific reason she needed help.

Debt

The widow's late husband had left her facing a large debt and their creditor was threatening to take the widow's two sons as slaves to work off the debt. In other words, she had serious financial problems which threatened the lives of her two sons. In that day, the creditor was legally allowed to "confiscate" a debtor until the debt was settled—so the creditor was within his rights. But she couldn't stand the thought of losing her sons.

Debt was not a dishonor to this honorable man. Most Christians today carry some debt in the form of a mortgage, at least. So the prophet's debt was not a black mark against him. He apparently was paying it off, but when he died, the widow had no ability to keep making the payments. In other words, bad things can happen to good people—then and now. We don't get a free pass on trouble just because we fear the Lord.

Destitution

But the widow's situation gets worse: She was destitute, on the verge of starvation. All she had left in her house was a single jar of oil (2 Kings 4:2). Here, Elisha's heart for this widow's situation was like the heart of God. He had genuine compassion on her, just as God did.

The Old Testament is filled with references to God's care for the orphan, the widow, and the poor. Psalm 68:5 says God is "a father of the fatherless, a defender of widows." Psalm 146:9 says, "The Lord watches over the strangers; He relieves the fatherless and widow" (see also Isaiah 1:17; Jeremiah 7:6). What is true of God was true of God's prophet, Elisha—and it should be true of us as well when it comes to those in need. That heart is evident through the food-relief programs sponsored by many churches to reach those outside the church and benevolence programs to help those in the church family.

The Command

Not unusual for a prophet, Elisha's command to the widow is a bit counterintuitive, not what one might expect (2 Kings 4:3-4). He tells the widow to go and borrow empty jars from all her neighbors —lots of them—and bring them into her house. She is then to pour the oil from her jar into the empty jars she has borrowed.

What would you have thought if you were in the widow's place? She has one nearly empty jar in her house, and now she has lots of empty jars. How is this helping with her debt problem? Even if it works—even if her oil is able to be multiplied to fill all the empty jars with oil—how is this a solution?

It's a faith situation on three counts (faith that requires action). First, she has to have faith that her neighbors will give her their empty jars. Second, she has to believe that the oil in her jar will expand to fill all the empty jars with oil. And third, she has to believe she and her sons can do this on their own, without Elisha—for Elisha told her to bring the empty jars inside her house and shut the door behind her.

The Commitment

As she and her sons began to pour their oil into the empty jars, it turns out to be just enough to fill every jar. "So the oil ceased" (2 Kings 4:6).

By any test, this is a miracle. God has altered the physical world to accomplish something that will meet the widow's need. One jar of oil multiplies itself and becomes enough oil to fill numerous empty jars. The oil stopped multiplying when the last jar was filled. It's as if the miracle extended to the degree of the widow's faith. She had x-number of jars to fill; she acted in faith; that's how much oil was produced. Her works (gathering the jars and pouring the oil) were consistent with the size of the miracle.

Her commitment to Elisha's instruction reveals an important principle: Faith is a verb. Faith isn't a warm feeling, attitude, or emotion. Faith is something you do. We demonstrate faith by our actions, our works. Our faith is manifested when we obey and act. That's at the heart of Hebrews 11, the famous Hall of Faith chapter that relates stories of Old Testament saints who acted in faith on God's instruction and His promises.

Real faith grabs hold of truth, of God's promises, and responds in action. James 2:14-26 declares that faith without works is dead. That makes obedience a synonym, of sorts, for faith. The only way we know if we have faith is if we step out in faith and act. Without actions, we have to ask ourselves what our faith is really for.

The Conclusion

In 2 Kings 4:7, the widow understands the point of this exercise (she had probably figured it out already). Elisha told her to take the numerous jars of oil and sell them. With the proceeds, she could pay her debt and use what was left for her and her sons' needs.

There are at least three principles that this anatomy, this analysis, of the miracle provide for us—principles that we can apply to our life of faith today.

The Principle of Personal Desperation

In verse 1, we read that the widow "cried out to Elisha." I love that phrase—"cried out"! It occurs in the Bible sixty different times. That tells me that there were a lot of needy people—no, desperate people—who didn't just pray to God, they cried out to God in their time of need.

When I was recovering from cancer, I went to New York City to preach at the Brooklyn Tabernacle. The one thing I remember most about that experience was the number of people who came up to me after the service and said they had been "crying out to God" for me as I battled my illness. I don't recall anyone telling me that before, but "crying out to God" is standard operating procedure at the famed Tuesday night prayer meetings at the Brooklyn Tabernacle. I was so blessed by what they were doing on my behalf before God.

The more desperate we are, the more likely we are to cry out to God. When things in life need a slight adjustment, we pray. When things are desperate, we need to cry out! Psalm 34:17 says, "The righteous cry out, and the Lord hears, and delivers them out of all their troubles."

Psalm 56:9 says, "When I cry out to You, then my enemies will turn back."

Psalm 57:2 says, "I will cry out to God Most High, to God who performs all things for me."

Psalm 107:28 says, "Then they cry out to the Lord in their trouble, and He brings them out of their distresses."

To whom are we crying out? To the God who is able to supply all our need "according to His riches in glory by Christ Jesus" (Philippians 4:19). How abundant is the supply of "His riches in glory"? Do you think it is sufficient to meet your need? Was God able to meet the widow's need with just one small jar of oil? How big is your need compared to God's "riches in glory"? More than adequate, I would say.

God is waiting for us to cry out to Him. As Jesus told His disciples, "If you then, being evil, know how to give good gifts to your children, how much more will your heavenly Father give the Holy Spirit to those who ask Him!" (Luke 11:13) Thinking we could exhaust the riches and provision of God is like thinking we could exhaust the amount of fresh water in a large lake. Our individual, daily need for water wouldn't make a "dent" in the water content of a large lake. Such a resource would be inexhaustible, for all practical purposes.

So it is with God's "riches in glory by Christ Jesus." What you need in a desperate situation is like a grain of sand compared to God's ability to meet your need.

The Principle of Divine Cooperation

In the miracle of the widow's oil, Elijah provided the instructions, but the widow was responsible to carry them out. There was God's part and the widow's part. It was an illustration of the principle of divine cooperation. God says what is true and we work out that truth in our own lives.

In one of Elijah's miracles, the prophet asked a widow to make him a meal with the small amount of flour and oil she had. She didn't see how it was possible, but as soon as she began preparing the meal, the flour and oil never ran out (1 Kings 17:16). Her job was to follow the instructions God gave her through Elijah. When she did, a miracle occurred.

On one occasion, Jesus' disciples had fished all night with no success. The next morning, Jesus told them where and how to let their nets down again. When they reluctantly obeyed, they caught so many fish their nets were breaking; they had to call for another boat to come and help land their catch. Even then, the catch was almost more than the two boats could get to shore (Luke 5:6-7). Would it have been possible for the disciples to make that catch without obeying Jesus' instructions? No. The instruction was a test of their faith.

Jesus tied a miracle to a condition of faith on many occasions (Mark 5:34, 36; 9:23). He told a blind man to go wash the mud off his eyes, which Jesus had placed there in the pool of Siloam. When he did, he came back with his sight (John 9:7-11). One of the most haunting passages in the New Testament is Mark 6:5-6—Jesus did not perform many miracles in Nazareth because of the peoples' unbelief.

On another occasion in the Old Testament, when Israel was ready to cross the Jordan River into the Promised Land of Canaan, God told the Levites to carry the Ark of the Covenant into the river and He would part the water. Step in *first,* then the waters would be parted. The river was at flood stage, flowing swiftly, but as soon as the priests' feet touch the water's edge, the river stopped and the people went across on dry ground (Joshua 3). Step *first,* then you'll see the miracle.

The principle of divine cooperation says that I must do what God tells me to do. God's part often follows our part. When we have a need and are crying out to the Lord, we need to see if there is some act of obedience that we need to act on.

The Principle of Potential Limitation

This principle is a fascinating part of this story: God's generosity to the widow extended as far as her capacity to receive. That is, His provision was limited only by the number of jars she collected. The principle says: If you want more oil, collect more jars!

This is an Old Testament illustration of the words of Jesus in Matthew 9:29: "According to your faith let it be to you." If you say, "I want God to bless me," the next question is, "How much do you want God to bless you?"

We have experienced this principle in our church. Our church produces an annual budget like most churches. Many years ago, we began a faith exercise of adding five percent to the previous year's budget when planning the next year's budget—and we trusted God to provide for that new level of ministry. And it always happened. We never outspent our income, even though every year our planned budget was five percent more than the previous year's. Looking back, it seems that five percent was the measure of our faith. And God provided according to our faith.

Somewhere along the way, we decided to plan for more than five percent of the previous year's budget. And every year God continues to provide that increased amount. As our faith grew, God's provision grew along with it. We have always had more than the budget requires. According to our faith, God has provided.

I would challenge you to grow your faith and trust God to provide. If you want more from God, trust God for more. And don't be disappointed if God doesn't provide what you want. Ask yourself, did He provide according to my faith?

The most important need that any of us have is in spiritual provision, and this principle comes into play there as well. Just as the widow had a debt to pay, we have a debt for sin that we can never repay. And just as God met the widow's need, He has paid our debt as well. But there is a condition: "Whoever calls on the name of the Lord shall be saved" (Romans 10:13). If we will trust God to forgive our debt by calling on the name of Christ, we will be forgiven—our debt will be paid. It's not enough to believe the facts of the Gospel, we must call upon the name of the Lord. According to our faith, it will be done for us. Have you called upon the name of the Lord by faith?

PERSONAL QUESTIONS

1. The Bible mentions caring for widows and orphans in multiple places.

   a. With what other sins did Jeremiah compare neglecting widows and orphans? (Jeremiah 7:1-11, especially verse 6)

   b. What did God say He would do if the leaders of Israel ignored widows and orphans? (Isaiah 1:15-17)

   c. How should God's attitude toward widows and orphans in the Old Testament affect the Church today? (James 1:27)

d. What do you think James meant by "pure and undefiled religion"?

e. Does this dimension of God's heart enter your sphere of influence very often? Does your church have financial or practical ministry opportunities to widows?

2. Describe a need you have at the present time that you are praying about.

a. Would you say you are praying about it or crying out to God about it? What separates the two?

b. What is your part in meeting that need? (Think of the widow gathering jars, pouring oil, etc.) That is, what steps are you taking in faith to see the need be realized?

c. What is God's part in this need—something only He can do?

3. Read Romans 10:9.

   a. What is man's part in salvation cited in this verse?

   b. What is God's part? What can only God do in saving a soul?

GROUP QUESTIONS

1. Read 2 Kings 4:1-7 as a group.

   a. What can we learn from the widow's boldness in asking for help?

   b. How comfortable are you asking fellow believers to pray for you in a time of need?

   c. How comfortable are you asking for help in practical, tangible ways? Why are we so hesitant to ask for assistance when we need help?

   d. Should it matter whether the need arises through fault, or no fault, of one's own? (Did Elisha quiz the widow about the reason for her family's debt?)

e. Should shame over the cause of a need keep us from approaching God? How does Hebrews 4:16 help in this regard?

f. How does the cause of another's need (foolishness, sin, negligence) impact our willingness to help? Does it change the kind of help we are willing to give?

2. Read Jesus' story in Luke 18:1-8.

   a. How often did the widow approach the judge? (verse 5)

   b. Why did the judge finally help her? (verse 5)

c. In what way did Elisha's widow and the widow in Jesus' story act the same? (See "cry out" in 2 Kings 4:1 and Luke 18:7.)

d. Can you share a time when you cried out to God in need?

e. Is there a difference between normal prayer and crying out to God?

DID YOU KNOW?

The practice of servitude as a form of debt repayment was allowed in Israel as a provision of the Mosaic law (Leviticus 25:35-46). But the entire process was governed by two guidelines. First, the backdrop of the practice was the fact that all of Israel had once been enslaved in the land of Egypt and treated harshly until God delivered them through Moses. Therefore, no Israelite, while repaying a debt, was to be treated as a slave, rather as a hired person until the debt was repaid. Second, regardless of when the person entered the condition of servitude, they were to be released on the Year of Jubilee (every fiftieth year) even if the debt remained unsettled. That was a year in which debts were forgiven, land was restored, and the land was allowed to rest.

The Ups and Downs of Life

2 Kings 4:8-37

In this lesson we witness the power of God in the valley of the shadow of death.

OUTLINE

The goodness of God is revealed in both the high points and the low points of life. Sometimes God's blessings occur as a show of His goodness and love. And sometimes they occur as a miracle to solve a critical problem. In both cases, His presence and power reflect who He is.

I. When God Delights You . . . Enjoy Him

II. When God "Disappoints" You . . . Seek Him

III. When God Delivers You . . . Thank Him

A. Miracles Are About Problems

B. Miracles Are More Than About Problems

OVERVIEW

Life is filled with good days and bad days, high points and low points, mountain peaks and deep valleys—even for Christians. We are not immune to the ups and downs of life, nor were the heroes of the biblical stories. Elijah, Job, Joseph, John the Baptist, Peter the disciple, the apostles Paul and John—all experienced the highs and lows of life—even the Lord Jesus Himself.

In this lesson from the life of the prophet, Elisha, we will meet a prosperous and godly woman who nonetheless experienced the lowest of lows, then back to the highest of highs.

The story begins in a small city called Shunem, about fifteen miles from Mount Carmel where Elisha was stationed. In Shunem was a notable woman—hospitable, wealthy, gracious, and good. Her home served as a rest-stop for Elisha as he traveled about the region. She and her husband even prepared a guest room for Elisha where he could stay overnight when he visited them (2 Kings 4:9-10). (The modern expression "prophet's chamber"—a guest room or home provided for visiting missionaries and speakers—is based on this woman's generous provision for Elisha.)

Little did this woman know that her generous hospitality would set in motion a series of events that would change her life dramatically.

WHEN GOD DELIGHTS YOU... ENJOY HIM

On one occasion when Elisha and his servant, Gehazi, were visiting Shunem and staying with the woman and her husband, Elisha asked what he might do for her to repay her hospitality (verse 13). Being well-to-do, she said they had everything they needed. But Gehazi observed to Elisha that they had no son and her husband was aged. So Elisha called the woman to his room and prophesied over her: "About this time next year you shall embrace a son" (verse 16). Understandably, the woman was skeptical. But just as Elisha prophesied, she became pregnant and gave birth to a son.

She was not the only woman this happened to in biblical history—God quickening a barren womb. Sarah, Abraham's wife, was the first. She gave birth to her first son, Isaac, at nearly one hundred years of age. Then Rebekah was childless for twenty years of marriage before birthing the twins, Esau and Jacob. Then Rachel, Jacob's wife, was childless until birthing Joseph. Manoah's wife was childless until she birthed Samson, the same with Hannah until she birthed Samuel. In the New Testament era, Elizabeth gave birth to John (the Baptist) well past the age of childbearing. And though she was very young, Mary, the mother of Jesus, bore a child without "knowing" a man—by the power of the Holy Spirit.

All the children born to the women just mentioned became key players in biblical history. But the child born to the Shunammite woman remains anonymous; we know nothing about him other than what is mentioned in this story. The birth of her son was definitely a high point, which became a low point, then again, a high point. The birth of her son and his ultimate restoration to her seem to play no significant role other than being evidence of God's desire to bless His children with good and perfect gifts (James 1:17; 1 Timothy 6:17).

Philip Ryken put it this way: "Some people live in the suspicion that God is out to get them. They do not believe that God is good all the way through. Instead, they think God is like a giant apple: beautiful, crisp, and tasty on the outside, but mealy and bitter somewhere near the core. They keep waiting for disaster to strike or judgment to fall. The truth is that God is good all the way through. It is his very nature to be good. He is good, has been good and always will be good. He cannot be anything but good."[1]

In the midst of the ups and downs of life, we should look out for God's unexpected gifts of grace and goodness. His goodness is often what sustains us through the low points of life. When you experience His goodness, give Him thanks for it—and enjoy it! It's been my observation through the years that some Christians have a hard time enjoying the blessings of God. Don't be one of those people! Enjoy the blessings of God every day.

When God "Disappoints" You... Seek Him

A family of two has become a family of three: the woman, her aged husband, and their young son. Several years pass and they experience the valley of the shadow of death. Their young son was in the fields with his father and was taken ill. He was returned home to his mother where he died a few hours later. She took the lifeless body of her young son and laid it on the bed in Elisha's room (2 Kings 4:18-21).

We don't know why the child died, only that he did. And this event illustrates the sometimes-unexplainable low points of life. In her despair, the woman traveled to Mount Carmel to seek help from Elisha. Upon arriving, she poured out her heart to the prophet. Elisha must have been perplexed. The woman hadn't asked for a child, but he prophesied the gift of God that would come to her. And now the gift has been taken away; the child has died (verses 27-28).

This is not the only time such a thing has happened; perhaps it has happened to you. You attempt to help someone and your actions backfire—and you have no idea why or what to do to fix things. Instead of saying, "I understand what you're going through," sometimes the best thing to do is to admit our lack of understanding.

"Elisha shows much wisdom in dealing with this distress. He didn't have an answer and he was honest about that. Some Christians assume they have a gift for always knowing the solution to the distresses of others, and they would do well to catch Elisha's humility and be quiet. Often, we don't have a clue about what God is up to in some believer's trouble. How liberating to confess: God has hidden it from me and has not informed me."[2]

What do we do in such a situation? We rely on what we do know: God is love and God is good. Even if the reasons for things are hidden from us, they are not hidden from God. And we rely on the fact that He knows, and if He wants us to know, He will reveal it to us in due time. But we take the path *toward* Him, not *away* from Him when things are difficult. The best way to move toward God is through His Word. Regardless of our circumstances, His Word remains true and just and right; it tells us all we need to know about God even if it doesn't tell us about ourselves and our circumstances.

When God Delivers You... Thank Him

So when God delights us, we enjoy Him. When He "disappoints" us, we seek Him. Finally, when God delivers us, we thank Him.

Elisha sent Gehazi ahead to the woman's house in Shunem with instructions to lay Elisha's staff on the dead boy's body. But there was no response. When Elisha arrived, he acted like a prophet, doing what no one would have expected. First, he prayed, then he laid down on top of the boy's body, face to face. The boy's body grew warm, but still no response. Elisha rose, walked around the house, and returned to the boy's bed and repeated the action—he stretched himself out on the child's body again. This time, the child sneezed seven times and opened his eyes (verses 33-36).

The boy's birth had been a miracle and his rebirth, back to life, was a miracle as well. Perhaps this is the story the writer of Hebrews referenced: "Through faith.... women received their dead raised to life again" (Hebrews 11:33, 35). The woman came in and bowed at Elisha's feet with gratitude—and took up her son and carried him downstairs (verse 37).

The New Living Translation of verse 37 says she was "overwhelmed with gratitude." Are we always "overwhelmed with gratitude" when God meets our need or answers our prayers? Do we remember to thank Him for His goodness and grace? The late author Lewis Smedes captured the essence of gratitude, reflecting on his recovery from a medical condition: "It was then that I learned that gratitude is the best feeling I would ever have, the ultimate joy of living. It was better than . . . winning a lottery, better than watching your daughter graduate from college, better and deeper than any other feeling; it is, perhaps the genesis of all other really good feelings in the human repertoire. . . . I am sure that nothing in life can ever match the feeling of being fully, totally, completely grateful."[3] We need to experience that feeling often, even daily. We have reason to. Every day, there are things we can be grateful for.

Elijah raised a widow's son in Zarephath. Elisha raised a woman's son in Shunem. And if we fast-forward to Luke 7, we find Jesus encountering the funeral procession of a boy who died in the village of Nain, not far from Shunem. The widow of Nain received her boy back from the dead when Jesus, the greatest Prophet, returned him to his mother. In all three cases, the sting was taken away from death by the goodness of God (1 Corinthians 15:55-57).

Let's reflect on two truths we can draw from the Elisha and the Shunammite woman's son.

Miracles Are About Problems

Here is a simple fact: When the woman's son was living, she didn't need a miracle. When he died, a miracle was her only hope. As far as I can tell, the Bible's miracles are about solving a problem.

If Pharaoh had let the Hebrew slaves go, there would have been no need for the miracles of the ten plagues. If the Egyptian army hadn't pursued them, there would have been no need for the parting of the Red Sea. All the way through the Old Testament, miracles happened as a remedy for a problem.

The same is true in the New Testament. The Gospel of John records seven miracles that Jesus did, all in response to a problem. First, the provision of wine at a wedding in Cana. Second, a nobleman's son was healed of a serious illness. Third, a man paralyzed for 38 years was healed. Fourth, a crowd of thousands of people needed food to eat and Jesus multiplied bread and a few fish to feed them with twelve baskets of leftovers. Fifth, Jesus stilled a storm on the Sea of Galilee that threatened to swamp the boat they were in. Sixth, Jesus healed a man who had been blind from birth. And seventh, Jesus raised His friend Lazarus from the dead.

Seven problems needed seven miracles, and they happened. If you and I don't have any problems, then we don't need a miracle from God. But if we do have a problem, we are a candidate for a miracle. Instead of being discouraged by the problem we face, we should remember our Bible history and realize that problems are what manifest the miracles of God. Can God do miracles today? Job said, "I know that you can do all things; no purpose of yours can be thwarted" (Job 42:2, NIV). Jeremiah 32:17 says, "There is nothing too hard for You." And Jesus said, "With God all things are possible" (Matthew 19:26), and "The things which are impossible with men are possible with God" (Luke 18:27).

God is the God of the impossible; nothing is too hard for Him. When anyone asks me if I believe in God doing miracles today, I say "Yes!" I've witnessed several miracles and heard about others. But we need to remember: We can't schedule God's miracles according to our timetable. God is not obligated to do miracles for us. Sometimes He wants us to learn that His grace is sufficient for us (2 Corinthians 12:7-10). Never stop believing in the God of all miracles. Just trust Him to do what is perfect for you.

Miracles Are More Than About Problems

Yes, miracles are about problems, but they are about *more* than problems. The reason the Gospel of John calls Jesus' miracles "signs" is that they are signposts to teach us something. Yes, the miracles solved a problem, but they also had something to show us about

God. And the apostle John explains their purpose: "And truly Jesus did many other signs in the presence of His disciples, which are not written in this book; but these are written that you may believe that Jesus is the Christ, the Son of God, and that believing you may have life in His name" (John 20:30-31).

So one of the purposes of Jesus' miracles was to show us who He was—the Son of God who came to give us new life, now and for eternity. Only the Son of God could do what Jesus did. Therefore His miracles were signs pointing to His divinity.

God continues to do miracles, signs, today that continue to point to the power and deity of Jesus Christ. In fact, the greatest miracle of all happens every day all over the world: the salvation and transformation of a human life! Millions of lives have been changed by the miracle of the new birth when nothing else had been able to effect that change. Only the miracle-working power of God could do it. If your life has been changed by Christ, then you are living proof that God still does miracles today.

When my wife, Donna, and I attended the fiftieth anniversary celebration of the church we started in Indiana, we visited with many people who I had led to Christ. Those lives were miracles, to be sure. But to see their children and grandchildren walking with the Lord—that was even more of a miracle. It shows how God continues to work miracles every day on planet Earth by transforming lives through faith in Christ.

But the most important question to ask is this: Have you experienced the miracle of the new birth in your own life? Are you evidence that God is working miracles today? If you are evidence of that miracle, then you have every reason to trust Him to continue to work miracles in your life when they are needed. You are the living proof! Nothing is impossible for God!

The next time you have a problem, look in the mirror and say, "God worked a miracle in my life once. I believe He can do it again." And then trust Him.

Notes

1. Philip Graham Ryken, *2 Kings* (Phillipsburg, NJ: P & R Publishing, 2019), 74.
2. Dale Ralph Davis, *2 Kings* (Great Britain: Christian Focus Publications Ltd., 2018), 67.
3. Lewis Smedes, *A Pretty Good Person: What It Takes to Live with Courage, Gratitude, and Integrity* (San Francisco: Harper San Francisco, 1990), 7.

PERSONAL QUESTIONS

1. Read James 1:2-5, 17.

   a. What is the significance of the word "when" in verse 2 (as opposed to "if")? What does "when" say about the likelihood of lows in life?

   b. What comes down to us from God? (verse 17)

   c. What do life's low points (trials) contribute to our life? (verses 3-4)

   d. Given that hard times produce maturity, why should we consider them as gifts of God?

   e. What did Elisha do when faced with the death of the child (2 Kings 4:33) that mirrors the admonition in James 1:5?

f. How does Romans 8:28-29 provide a backdrop for the benefits of low points in our life?

g. How is verse 28 connected to verse 29? That is, how is God's "purpose" (verse 28) described in verse 29? What is God's ultimate purpose to which life's lows contribute?

2. Read 1 Timothy 6:17.

   a. What does God provide for us to enjoy? (Use blessings in your life as examples.)

   b. How should we balance using God's blessings for our enjoyment with the suffering in the world? How do you balance these two realities in your own life?

3. What do you admire about Elisha as he ministered to the widow in her time of need?

GROUP QUESTIONS

1. Share the way you view your life: mostly highs? mostly lows? a balance?

    a. One of Job's friend's said life was what? (Job 5:7) Job saw life as what? (Job 14:1) Were they being pessimistic or realistic?

    b. How easy is it to allow our circumstances to color how we view life and God?

    c. How do we avoid letting circumstances determine our perspective on life and God?

    d. What does James 1:17 say about God, His gifts, and His character?

2. What would you tell a friend who needed a miracle in his or her life?

a. What lessons can we draw from Paul's experience in 2 Corinthians 12:7-10?

b. Which is the greater miracle: an *actual* miracle or the miracle of making it through a trial by the grace of God (in the way Paul did)? Why is the latter as much a miracle as the former?

3. Share about the unexpected gifts of God's goodness in your life. How do these gifts provide balance to the low times in life?

4. Why is admitting "I don't know the answer" acceptable in a difficult situation?

a. Why should we move *toward* God in those moments?

b. Why should we not move *away* from God in those moments?

DID YOU KNOW?

While all four Gospel accounts of Christ's life and ministry describe His miracles, only John's Gospel makes a point of designating them as signs. In that way, John's Gospel stands apart from the other three "synoptic" Gospels (*synoptic* is from the word synopsis or summary). Matthew, Mark, and Luke present a chronological account of Christ's life, while John presents a thematic, or theological, account structured around seven key miracles. John calls the miracles signs ("signs" appears seventeen times in John's Gospel), saying there were many other signs Jesus did which he didn't include (John 20:30: 21:25). The signs he included in his Gospel were chosen because they point to the fact "that Jesus is the Christ" (John 20:31).

The Healing of Naaman

2 Kings 5:1-19

In this lesson we trace the circuitous route that led to two miracles in a soldier's life.

OUTLINE

Miracles in the Bible seem to have two purposes—at least implied, if not stated explicitly. One is to solve a problem in the life of a person or people. But the other is to point that person or people to the God of the miracle. Miracles have a temporal and eternal purpose.

I. **The Commander's Condition**

II. **The Commander's Captive**

III. **The Commander's Correspondence**

IV. **The Commander's Cure**

V. **The Commander's Conversion**

VI. **The Commander's Crisis**

VII. **Conclusion**
   A. The Progression of This Miracle
   B. The Promotion of This Miracle
   C. The Point of This Miracle

OVERVIEW

We don't hear as much about leprosy as in times past—especially biblical times. But as we continue our study of the life and ministry of the prophet Elisha, we will learn about a prominent man who had leprosy. He was a man who needed what in that day could only be a miracle cure. And he found that cure when he met Elisha.

The story begins outside Israel, in Syria, the home Naaman, "commander of the army of the king of Syria . . . a great and honorable man in the eyes of his master" (2 Kings 5:1).

The Commander's Condition

From 2 Kings 5:1 we learn six things about this impressive man, Naaman. He was important, great, honorable, victorious, mighty, and courageous. He was an impressive man—the equivalent today of the Chief of Staff of the armed forces. Interestingly, we also see that "by him the Lord had given victory to Syria." (This may refer to an unnamed victory of Syria over the Assyrians who were the enemies of Israel.) But the last three words of the verse cast a shadow on this man's life: "But [he was] a leper."

One thing in our lives can overshadow all the other good things if we let it. Like when I went for a physical in my forties and was told I was fine . . . except for a mass in my abdomen they needed to check. That mass turned out to be lymphoma cancer. All the other good health points were forgotten at that moment. It was the same with Naaman—he was "all good," a military hero, except for a little thing called leprosy.

Many people experience that "except" moment in their lives today. They have achieved all the success the world has to offer, except for one thing: They don't know God. They may not have a physical condition called leprosy or cancer, but they have the "sickness" of sin. That one thing can negate all the other positive things in life. If you don't have God, nothing else matters.

The Commander's Captive

Like life sometimes does, Naaman's story takes an interesting and unexpected twist. His army had been in the field on raids and they brought back a young woman, a captive from "the land of Israel" (2 Kings 5:2). She became a servant to Naaman's wife. This young girl told Naaman and his wife about Elisha the prophet, how "he would heal [Naaman] of his leprosy" (verse 3).

We don't know who this young woman was. She had been kidnapped by the Syrian army and taken from her homeland and family to serve Naaman in Syria. But she became a source of light, a witness to the power of God, in her captive setting. She reminds us of the story of the young Jewess, Esther, who was in Persia at just the right time to save the Jews from genocide (Esther 4:14). God put her in Naaman's life to be a link between his disease and a cure. She was as courageous to speak up as Naaman was to lead armies in battle.

The Commander's Correspondence

As a man of action, Naaman went to his king and told him of this amazing development. The king told Naaman to go to the prophet immediately. He wrote a letter of introduction for Naaman to take to the king of Israel along with gifts: 750 pounds of silver, 150 pounds of gold, and ten sets of clothing suitable for royalty. His letter asked for help in healing Naaman of his leprosy (2 Kings 5:4-6). (These gifts would have been worth millions of dollars in today's money.)

The story so far seems straightforward—but it gets complicated. For whatever reason, the letter from the king of Syria to the king of Israel failed to mention Elisha as the one Naaman needed to see. So when the king of Israel got the letter, he thought he was being made responsible to heal Naaman. He thought the king of Syria was setting him up to fail and thus become a target of recriminations (2 Kings 5:7). King Joram thought his failure would result in Israel being attacked by Syria.

King Joram exclaimed, "Am I God?" In other words, "Can I do what only God can do? Why does the king of Syria expect me to do what only God can do?" His failure was to forget that the God of Israel can do what no man can do. He had taken his eyes off God. What a contrast with the simple slave girl who believed God, through His prophet, could heal Naaman. She had faith that the king of Israel lacked.

The Commander's Cure

Somehow, word got to Elisha about the king of Israel being so upset; he sent a message to Joram: "Please let [Naaman] come to me, and he shall know that there is a prophet in Israel" (2 Kings 5:8). This message was delivered to Naaman, and he made his way to Elisha's house. When Naaman arrived, Elisha gave him instructions through a servant: "Go and wash in the Jordan seven times, and your flesh shall be restored to you, and you shall be clean" (2 Kings 5:10).

Naaman flew into a rage! He was not used to dealing with a prophet of God. He felt Elisha's instructions were simplistic; he expected a personal audience with the prophet where some healing rituals would be performed and make him well. Besides, why should he come all the way into Israel to wash in the Jordan River? Surely the rivers of Damascus are better than the rivers of Israel. Surely, he could have washed in them and been made well (2 Kings 5:11-12).

Naaman thought he knew better. He was seriously ill, but thought he knew better than the prophet who had a track record of healing people. And why should he have to bathe in the muddy Jordan River instead of one of the clear mountain rivers in Syria? None of this made sense to the great military man, Naaman.

What Naaman didn't understand was that God heals and saves on His terms, not ours. We need to remember that as much as Naaman needed to learn it. Dale Ralph Davis captures this lesson perfectly: "We are not so far from Naaman. We set up in our minds what we think God should or should not do, and when he apparently fails to toe our particular line, we feel a sense of grievance. Naaman fits this mold; perhaps we do as well. We not only want God's benefit, but we also want to specify the way in which he must bring it. So the sovereign God has become our errand boy."[1]

Thankfully, Naaman was corrected by his servants. They presented him with a perceptive question: If Elisha had told you to do something heroic or pretentious, you would have done it immediately. How much more, then, should you do this simple thing of bathing in the Jordan (2 Kings 5:13)? Naaman saw their point and went and washed seven times in the Jordan and was completely healed of his leprosy (verse 14).

As if that miracle had not been enough, there was yet another miracle to come to the commander of Syria's armies.

The Commander's Conversion

Naaman was not just cured from his skin disease, he was cured of his sin disease. He was converted from his unbelief. He and his servants returned from the river to Elisha's house where Naaman confessed the supremacy of Israel's God. And he offered Elisha a gift for his services of healing—which the prophet refused (2 Kings 5:15-16).

In New Testament terms, we would say this was the moment of Naaman's conversion, the moment of him being born again. Elisha refused Naaman's gift as a matter of integrity. But his refusal is a type of New Testament truth: There is no way to pay for the grace of God that brings salvation into our life. No good deeds can atone for bad deeds. Salvation is the gift of God alone (Ephesians 2:8-9). We can only be saved, healed, made whole, and delivered by receiving God's grace and favor by faith. It's so we can have nothing about which to boast, so God alone receives the credit and glory.

Naaman's story is one of the great conversion stories of the Bible. Many powerful and gifted people today need to learn what Naaman learned: God's gifts come only by His grace through faith.

The Commander's Crisis

The end of this story is strange, but important, and we need to note it. In verses 17-19, Naaman makes two requests: First, that he be allowed to load two mules with dirt from where Elisha lived, on which he can offer sacrifices to God when he returns to Syria. Second, that he be forgiven ahead of time for accompanying his king into the temple of the god Rimmon in Syria. He will have to bow before Rimmon with his king, but in his heart he won't mean it.

The dirt wasn't just a souvenir. He was serious; he wanted to establish a little altar of sacrifice made of that dirt on which to worship the God of Israel who had healed him. And the second request is rather touching. He's a new believer wanting to make sure he wouldn't be sinning if he went into a temple of an idol as part of his job. Elisha's answer is equally touching. He tells Naaman, "It's okay." Instead of giving Naaman a legalistic set of rules to follow, he knew Naaman would work out the details of his new faith in time. If Naaman offended the king of Syria unnecessarily, it might cost him his job and his possible future influence on the king in spiritual matters.

There's a lot of wisdom here for us. Sometimes we burden new Christians down with lots of dos and don'ts about the Christian life—as if we don't trust the Holy Spirit to guide that person into all righteousness. That process is called sanctification—and it doesn't happen overnight. The best follow-up program, or discipleship program, I know of is called the local church. When a new Christian sits under good Bible teaching, participates in Spirit-led worship, gets in a small group with mature believers—God can begin to direct his or her steps off the old paths of life into the new paths of life. The old ways of life become uncomfortable and are slowly (sometimes quickly) discarded, replaced by new godly patterns of living.

I think that's what Elisha was doing with Naaman—sending him off under the care of God to work out his salvation going forward (Philippians 2:12).

Conclusion

There are three important lessons to take away from this story.

The Progression of This Miracle

This miracle proceeds along a circuitous route. It starts with a problem, an illness, and goes to a conversation with a young slave girl. Then the solution almost gets off track when the message between two kings is communicated poorly. When that gets straightened out, Naaman almost refuses the help he is looking for because of pride. Enter Naaman's servants—they wisely point out how Naaman needs to humble himself (in so many words) and receive the prophet's instruction. Finally, Naaman makes his way to the Jordan River and follows the prescription given by Elisha and is healed in both body and spirit.

It's true—sometimes a non-Christian will hear the Gospel and respond immediately. He or she places faith in Christ and is saved on the spot. Yes, that happens, but not usually in my experience. Normally, people hear or read a Gospel presentation—or they have an experience like the death of a friend or loved one. Something causes them to reflect and consider the claims of Christ or the reality of death and eternal life. Then, after consideration and conversations, the person decides to become a follower of Jesus.

For whatever reasons, that's usually the way salvation occurs. And we need to be patient with the progression that this miracle often follows.

The Promotion of This Miracle

At the center of this miracle story is a young woman taken captive in a foreign land. She lacked position, prominence, power; she had no status; she was on the lowest rung of the social scale in a foreign land. She could have been angry and bitter toward the man who had caused her to be a captive, especially since she now had to serve his wife every day. She could have thought, "Naaman has leprosy; serves him right! I'm not going to help him after what he has done to me." But she didn't do any of that. Instead of being bitter, she saw a way to help Naaman get better. She did what she thought God would want her to do. In short, she loved her enemy instead of hating her enemy (Matthew 5:43-48). In doing so, she changed Naaman's life and the lives of his family. Her actions resulted in the God of Israel being carried from Israel back to a pagan nation in the heart of a changed official.

We should never underestimate the impact of one simple act of humility or obedience. Like the young woman, we should always do the right thing and then trust the Lord to use it for good and His glory (Romans 8:28).

The Point of This Miracle

There were two miracles in this story: one, the miracle that cleansed Naaman's skin; the other, the miracle that cleansed Naaman's sins. His outer man was cleansed but so was his inner man. The lesser miracle was the healing of Naaman's disease; the greater miracle was the transformation of his whole life.

We see both dimensions of life in play in an event in Mark 2:1-12. A paralyzed man is brought to Jesus and He asks the religious leaders, Which is easier—to say the man's sins are forgiven or to heal him of his paralysis? Obviously, it's easier to say sins are forgiven because that can't be disproved. So Jesus did the harder—healing of his paralysis which could be instantly verified. So to prove He had the power to do the "easier" (forgive sins), He did the "harder" (healing).

But in reality, both things are impossible for man and only possible with God. When Naaman saw his leprosy was cured, he immediately was drawn to the harder thing: believing in the God of Israel. His body would break down and deteriorate in the grave one day, but his spirit would live forever with God. So the point of the miracle was to help Naaman see his need to believe in the one true God.

The miracles Jesus did were, of course, done compassionately to help people. But there was a larger point, as John wrote: to help people know that by believing in Jesus they could have eternal life (John 20:30-31). If you are a Christian today, you have experienced life's greatest miracle.

Note

1. Dale Ralph Davis, *2 Kings* (Great Britain: Christian Focus Publications Ltd., 2018), 90-91.

PERSONAL QUESTIONS

1. Read Genesis 45:5-7 and Esther 4:12-14.

   a. How do these two situations illustrate the importance of trusting God for where He has us at any moment in life?

   b. How did the life of a young captive woman in Syria in 2 Kings 5 put in motion a life-changing string of events? How might she have acted instead of how she did?

   c. List the places God has placed you at this time in your life. (home, work, etc.)

   d. Have you thought about *why* God has you there? Can you cite examples of seeds you have sown or are sowing in hopes of bringing about changes? Have you seen changes already?

e. Of all the places God has you, how many are "less than ideal" for you (like the servant girl)? Are you committed to sowing seeds of godliness anyway?

f. The servant girl was a link between God and Naaman. List the people for whom you may be that same kind of link.

2. How did Naaman almost miss his miracle because of his presuppositions about how the healing would happen? (2 Kings 5:10-14)

a. How easy is it for you to let God be God in your life?

b. To what lengths is God willing to go to break down our preconceived notions? (See Acts 9:1-19.)

GROUP QUESTIONS

1. Read 2 Kings 5:1-9 as a group. Why did the whole story of Naaman's miracle hang on the attitude of the servant girl?

    a. How might she have felt toward Naaman given the circumstances of her being in Syria?

    b. In what way did she fulfill Jesus' teaching in Matthew 5:43-48?

    c. How do her actions illustrate the spiritual principle of "do the next right thing" in situations where one doesn't know what to do?

    d. Share personal examples of sowing a seed of obedience that ends up bearing fruit later.

e. Why is Galatians 6:7 a reason to always do the generous, good, or righteous thing?

2. How do you feel about Elisha's permission to Naaman to accompany his king into the pagan temple? (2 Kings 5:18-19)

a. Share personal examples of how you learned to "take off the old" and "put on the new" after becoming a Christian. Are you still making that kind of progress today?

b. What is our tendency—especially when it comes to our children—when it comes to guiding new Christians to maturity? (Tell them vs. show them; force them vs. allow them?)

c. Why is the Holy Spirit's role in sanctification so important? Why is "one size fits all" not applicable when dealing with individual new Christians?

DID YOU KNOW?

Leprosy is an infectious disease of the skin that can lead to nerve damage and deterioration of afflicted limbs (fingers, toes). One of the chief dangers of leprosy is the gradual inability to feel pain in the afflicted area, meaning wounds can be unfelt and go untreated. Leprosy is spread by contact with an afflicted person, though it is not immediately contagious. Historically, lepers have been isolated from the general population in order to prevent contact and spread. This was true in the Old Testament where a significant set of guidelines for managing skin diseases was in place (Leviticus 13–14). Jesus was noted for touching and healing individuals with leprosy (Mark 1:40-42) and for dining in the home of "Simon the leper" in Bethany—possibly a former leper whom Jesus had healed (Matthew 26:6)

An Ordinary Miracle

2 Kings 6:1-7

In this lesson we discover that there is no need too small for God to meet.

OUTLINE

When we read the stories of miracles in the Bible, they often are about important people and large needs. To get the impression that God's intervention is limited to only those is wrong. God cares about the ordinary problems of ordinary people. And we are all ordinary people.

I. **God Cares About Ordinary People**

II. **God Cares About Ordinary Projects**

III. **God Cares About Ordinary Problems**

OVERVIEW

In the previous lesson, we found Elisha ministering the miracles of God to a V.I.P.—a very important person in the kingdom of Syria. He was a military man who had the king's confidence and the admiration of all who knew him. He was sick with leprosy, and God healed his body—but he also healed his heart, and the man put his faith in the God of Israel.

Does God only deliver miracles to V.I.P.s who have dramatic needs? What about ordinary people like you and me? I know—every person is important in God's sight, but somehow we think God pays more attention to "important" people. In this lesson about Elisha we find that God cares about ordinary people, ordinary projects, and ordinary problems.

By the time we get to 2 Kings 6, Elisha has performed at least ten different miracles, all rather extraordinary. Granted, no miracle is ordinary. But in this lesson, we find Elisha performing a miracle that is, by comparison, rather ordinary. But a miracle that reminds us that every person has His attention. It reminds us that God cares about the small things in life as well as the large things.

Dale Davis captures this perspective on God perfectly: "The greatness of God in large measure consists in the fact that he is faithful in the little things. We make a mistake when we confuse God's greatness with bigness or when we associate his greatness only with bigness. Part of our God's greatness appears in the fact that he does attend to the small problems, the seemingly mundane and ordinary affairs of his people's lives."[1]

God Cares About Ordinary People

As successor to the prophet Elijah, a prophetic movement developed and grew under Elisha. We don't know how many prophets there were, but the Lord's reference to seven thousand who had not bowed to Baal in Israel might have indicated the number of prophets (1 Kings 19:18). Regardless of the number, the size of the company of prophets living around Elisha grew to the extent that they needed increased space to live and meet (2 Kings 6:1).

Increased ministry, back then and today, requires increased space and facilities. It's why we build buildings, so the church can meet together with classroom space for the training of children, young people, and adults. The need for space is a good problem to have; it's a problem God is more than happy to help meet. Facilities are a means to an end—the goal is ministry and changed lives. Elisha recognized the need and agreed to the building project. When the end is consistent with God's purposes in the earth—the growth of the Church and expansion of the kingdom—He gets involved to help.

We are fast approaching a world population of eight billion souls. You and I are one individual out of almost eight billion people, a seemingly insignificant number. Yet in God's sight, we are not insignificant. Each person bears His image and has worth in His sight. The Bible says He knows the details of our life and the number of our days (Psalm 139:16). "Are not two sparrows sold for a copper coin? And not one of them falls to the ground apart from your Father's will. But the very hairs of your head are all numbered. Do not fear therefore; you are of more value than many sparrows" (Matthew 10:29-31).

The truth is, we are all ordinary people—all human beings, made in God's image, all of the same species. And the prophets in Elisha's school were ordinary people as well. So he cared about their need to have a place to meet and minster. And they would soon discover God cared about even the details involved in its construction.

It is amazing to think that the omniscient and omnipotent Creator-God of the universe cares about everything from the hairs on our head to the heads of state who are involved in international dealings between nations. He is the God of big things and small things and everything in between. Isaiah the prophet wrote,

> For thus says the High and Lofty One
> Who inhabits eternity, whose name is Holy:
> "I dwell in the high and holy place,
> With him who has a contrite and humble spirit,
> To revive the spirit of the humble,
> And to revive the heart of the contrite ones."
> Isaiah 57:15

The High and Lofty One revives the spirit of the humble and the heart of the contrite. We see that most clearly, of course, in the Person of Jesus Christ. He was no respecter of persons; He ministered to the religious leaders and the poor and downtrodden. He received people as they came to Him, not choosing one above another. He provided a miraculous touch for those in need regardless of class or standing.

God Cares About Ordinary Projects

Second Kings 6:2-4 reveals the ordinary project the prophets were undertaking: They needed to construct an enlarged space in which to meet and minister. The plan was to go to the Jordan River and cut trees with which to build their structure. And they wanted their leader, Elisha, to travel with them. Elisha approved the plan for the project and consented to go with them, so they set off. Arriving at their destination, they began to fell the trees they needed (verses 3-4).

Everything we undertake for God—from building a building, a family, a business, a life—if the plan is to build for the glory of God, we can be confident of His presence and help. That doesn't mean it will be easy. In fact, it likely will not be. But it will be faith-stretching, which is what we all need. I have never undertaken a building project for the Lord that was easy or that didn't require great faith. But He is always there to see it through.

The international evangelist, the late John Haggai, was well-known for his personal and ministry motto: "Attempt something so great for God, it's doomed to failure unless God be in it." If we could do something without God, we exclude the need for Him to work in our midst. When we build beyond our ability, we depend on God to step in and do what we can't. The key is keeping God involved every step of the way, never moving ahead of Him. The short story in James 4:13-15 says it all: If the Lord wills, we will do this and or that.

I have often been unclear about next steps when it came to building things. In such situations, there is only one thing to do: bow before the Lord and ask for His direction and help. In my experience, He has never failed to provide. The psalmist wrote, "Unless the Lord builds the house, they labor in vain who build it; unless the Lord guards the city, the watchman stays awake in vain" (Psalm 127:1).

The Lord cares about you and the projects you undertake for Him. If you keep the Lord by your side throughout your project, He will stay beside you and guide and provide all you need. If God has called you to do something for Him, He will provide. God never calls without providing the resources along the way.

God Cares About Ordinary Problems

The heart of this miracle comes in a rather pedestrian thing that happens—the equivalent of a broken tool used by one of the prophets. But Elijah's response shows that God cares about ordinary problems.

As one of the prophets was cutting a tree, his iron ax head fell into the water of the river. The story doesn't say the ax, but the ax head, as if it slipped off the handle of the ax and flew into the water. The prophet immediately voices two concerns: Number one, the tool has been lost; number two, the ax had been borrowed—it belonged to someone else (2 Kings 6:5).

Iron tools were rare in that day and time, and that means they were valuable. Imagine borrowing an expensive power tool from a friend and having it bounce out of the back of your pickup truck as you drive down the road. The reason the tool was borrowed is because the prophets lived on meager incomes. The prophet would have had no way to buy an expensive replacement tool to return to the owner of the original one. And that means he was in debt, and debtors could be consigned to servitude or slavery until the debt was paid. This was not a simple matter of losing a small screwdriver; it was an expensive tool, the loss of which created a significant debt.

Naturally, the prophet called for Elisha to help. And no one could have predicted what Elisha would do. He cut off a stick, threw it in the river, and the iron head floated to the surface (2 Kings 6:6-7)! And the prophet reached out and retrieved it from the water. He probably reattached it to the handle and returned to work.

This is such a simple story—only seven verses long in Scripture. It is Elisha's most ordinary miracle, to be sure. But it teaches us a lesson and a truth about God. When simple things arise in the life of God's ordinary people, He cares. Some will say this miracle never happened—that iron can't float. Neither can a world come into existence from nothing! So I believe God can do the complicated things and the simple things as well.

The hymnwriter, John Newton, who wrote "Amazing Grace," also wrote these words: "Not one concern of ours is small, if we belong to Him; to teach us this, the Lord of all once made iron to swim." Nothing is too small or too large for God.

These verses support that notion:

- Psalm 37:17—The Lord takes care of the godly.
- Psalm 55:22—Cast your cares on the Lord, and He will sustain you.
- Psalm 138:6—The Lord is great, but He cares for the humble.

Reading verses and stories in the Bible about God's helping nature is one way to increase your faith that He will help you. For example:

- 1 Samuel 7—The prophet Samuel led the Israelites in a victorious battle against the Philistines. Afterward he erected a stone monument and called it "Ebenezer," which means, "Thus far the Lord has helped us" (verse 12).
- 2 Chronicles 32:8—Years later, King Hezekiah encouraged the people against the invading Assyrians: "With us is the Lord our God, to help us and to fight our battles."
- Psalm 46:1—"God is our refuge and strength, a very present help in trouble."
- Hebrews 13:5-6—The Lord will never leave us; we will not fear what anyone can do to us.
- Hebrews 4:16—Mercy and grace to help are only a prayer away.

The Bible was given to all of us ordinary people. And as I mentioned above, we are all ordinary people with ordinary needs who are looked after by a great God. If I could bring an ax head from the bottom of the river to the surface, why would I need God? I don't know how or when He will choose to display His power and love in miraculous ways, but I don't need to know. I only need to know Him and to trust Him in all things. He has proven that He can help in a myriad of ways, so I am willing to trust Him to help me when I have a need.

Here is a story of how God worked once in my life: I met my wife, Donna, when we were both in college. After we graduated in 1963, we were married and headed out to begin training for the ministry at Dallas Theological Seminary. We didn't have much money at all, but found a tiny apartment to rent. We both got jobs pretty quickly, but failed to remember that when you begin a new job you usually don't get paid for two weeks after starting work. About halfway through the second week we ran out of money and food. We were determined not to ask our parents for help, so we would walk across the street to a grocery store and count out the change we had to buy the barest of staples.

One of the reasons we were so short on funds was that before leaving for Dallas I got a call from our bank saying my checking account was overdrawn by $800. We had been so rushed preparing everything for the wedding and honeymoon that I just assumed I had made a mistake and overdrawn the account. So I had to take $800 of the money we had set aside for starting life in Dallas and give it to the bank. That hurt!

But one day, during those first two weeks when we were just getting by, I arrived home from classes at seminary to find a letter from my bank. They apologetically explained that they had discovered an error in their accounting for my checking account. In the letter was a check for the $800 I had given them before we left! To me, that was a miracle! In human terms, it was an accounting error, but for me it was God knowing we were going to need that money. At just the right time, He provided it.

That's an ordinary story from two ordinary people. But it fits with God "resurrecting" an expensive tool for an ordinary prophet in Israel three thousand years ago. God is a big God who loves to do big things for ordinary people.

When I preached this series of messages on Elisha and his miracles, our nation was still trying to recover from the COVID-19 pandemic. Many people in our church had been out of work. Even though businesses were beginning to open back up, not everyone knew if their job would still be there. It was a time when ordinary people had very ordinary, but very personal, needs. I encouraged them then, as I encourage you now—God cares about those needs.

Even when life returns to "normal" in our economy—or the economies of nations around the world—other needs will arise. There is no end to the challenges we all face in life. We must live in the habit and practice of taking every need to God in prayer. He is the God who, from Genesis until today, has been meeting the needs of His people. Sometimes in dramatic ways, sometimes not. It doesn't matter how; it only matters that we bring our ordinary projects and problems to our great God.

Do you have a project or a problem facing you today? If you don't know where to turn, turn to God and lay it before Him. He cares for you and will respond to the smallest and greatest needs if you will trust Him.

Notes

1. Dale Ralph Davis, *2 Kings* (Great Britain: Christian Focus Publications Ltd., 2018), 104.
2. Alex and Stephen Kendrick, "God Knows Every Hair on Your Head," *Lifeway*, July 17, 2019, https://www.lifeway.com/en/articles/god-knows-every-hair-on-your-head-revealed-overcomer.

PERSONAL QUESTIONS

1. What does Psalm 139:13-16 tell you about God's knowledge of who you are—and your future?

2. Read Matthew 10:1-42.

   a. What is the context of Jesus' teaching about "the hairs of your head in verse 30"? Who was Jesus talking to and why?

   b. What "project" were Jesus' listeners involved in? (Matthew 10:1)

   c. What does that say about God's willingness to be involved in helping those who are doing His "work"?

   d. From a stewardship perspective, should there be any part of our life that is not about "God's work"? Therefore, is there any area of our life that God is not interested in supporting?

e. List the top five areas of stewardship responsibility you believe God has given you. And, list the most pressing need you have in each area. How could God meet these "ordinary" needs in your life?

3. Read James 4:13-15.

   a. How typical was the planning of the men in this story?

   b. What point is James making about involving God from the very start of our projects?

   c. How did Jesus illustrate this principle in His life? (See Luke 22:42; John 4:34; 5:19, 30.)

   d. Think about the "projects" in your life at the moment. Have you committed each one to God and asked for His guidance and direction?

GROUP QUESTIONS

1. Talk about the ways in which every area of life—marriage, parenting, work, ministry, recreation—is a "building project" that God can get behind.

   a. What would be the equivalent of a lost ax in any of these areas—seemingly small but vitally important? What should we do when something unexpected happens?

   b. How often do we stop and pray (ask God to be involved) in meeting the small needs that arise daily in these areas?

   c. What encouragement about prayer does Philippians 4:6-7 provide?

   d. What specific things does Hebrews 4:16 say God will provide when we come Him?

   e. What is the "grace" for in that verse? Grace to ______ in time of _______. How does grace help when we have a need?

   f. How did grace help Paul in 2 Corinthians 12:7-10?

2. What reasons does Scripture give for understanding we are ordinary, but not ordinary, at the same time?

   a. What reasons do you have for thinking God cares about you and your needs as much as He cares for "important" people?

   b. Has something happened in your life recently on the same scale as the "lost ax head" in this story? How did you react? How was the situation resolved? What did you learn?

DID YOU KNOW?

As an illustration of how God cares for us, Jesus said that the very hairs on our head are all numbered (Matthew 10:30). How many hairs would that represent? Alex and Stephen Kendrick did a bit of research on the subject and found that blondes have about 150,000 hairs; redheads have around 90,000 hairs, and those with black or brown hair have about 110,000 hairs on their head. If we average it out to about 100,000 hairs per head and use the figure of 7.6 billion "heads" on planet Earth, that means there are 7,660,000,000,000,000 (or 7.66 quadrillion) hairs that "have a number on them." Given that God keeps up with more stars than that in the universe, it seems doable for Him![2]

Experiencing God's Protection

2 Kings 6:8-23

In this lesson we discover the miracles of perception and prayer.

OUTLINE

The Bible speaks about the natural man—the person unaided by the Spirit of God who helps us see things from God's perspective. Once our perspective changes and we see the world through His eyes, we gain the courage to pray and expect God's solutions to our problems.

I. The Lord Protects Us in Unusual Ways

II. The Lord Protects Us in Unseen Ways

III. The Lord Protects Us in Unexpected Ways

IV. Conclusion

A. The Power of Perspective
B. The Possibilities of Prayer

OVERVIEW

One of the most amazing accounts of God's miraculous protection involved Corrie ten Boom who was taken prisoner, along with her sister, Betsie, by the Nazis and sent to a concentration camp. Corrie had hidden a Bible under her dress; she prayed that God would send angels to surround her and make her invisible to the guards so they would not search her. She passed through two different inspection points at the camp without being searched. The women in line in front of her and behind her were searched, but she was not.

I absolutely believe that God miraculously made the guards pass over her and not discover her Bible. I've never had a need for that kind of protection, but I have had the need for other types of protection—as I'm sure you have as well.

God is our protector! From Genesis to Revelation, God watched over His people, keeping them safe in the midst of danger. That doesn't mean that all were kept from bodily harm, even untimely death. But God was always there; He could have stopped any such event at any time. If He did, it was for His purposes; if He didn't, it was also for His purposes.

God told Abraham, "Do not be afraid, Abram. I am your shield" (Genesis 15:1). The psalmist wrote, "The Lord is my fortress, protecting me from danger, so why should I tremble?" (Psalm 27:1, NLT) Zechariah wrote, "The Lord of Heaven's Armies will protect his people" (Zechariah 9:15, NLT). Jesus prayed, "Father . . . now protect them by the power of your name" (John 17:11, NLT). And Peter wrote, "God is protecting you by his power" (1 Peter 1:5, NLT).

My wife and I once found ourselves in the midst of an angry group in Washington, D.C., who were bent on causing unrest and destruction in that city. We were trying to get back to our hotel and were completely blocked off. I prayed every step of the way for God's protection, and we eventually reached our destination safely. There are times when all of us need God's protection.

In this lesson from the life of Elisha, we will look at a series of miracles that were connected, arising from the need for God's protection. We will see that God protects in unusual ways, unseen ways, and unexpected ways.

The Lord Protects Us in Unusual Ways

The story begins in 2 Kings 6:8-10. Syria was making war against Israel. The king of Syria told his officers to set up a camp at a certain place. When Elisha learned the king's strategy, he sent word to the king of Israel—more than once—to avoid that place lest they run into the army of Syria. We don't know how Elisha came to learn the king of Syria's strategy, but it must have infuriated the king to discover that his plans had been leaked to the king of Israel.

Was there a mole in the Syrian camp, conveying information to Elisha? Did God allow Elisha to supernaturally hear or see the Syrian army's plans? We don't know. All we know is that God protected the Israelite army in an unusual way.

The Syrian king was enraged ("greatly troubled") by his plans being known by the Israelite king (verse 11). He called his officials together and demanded to know who was betraying him by leaking his plans. They denied being at fault and blamed Elisha: "Elisha, the prophet who is in Israel, tells the king of Israel the words that you speak in your bedroom" (verse 12).

This wasn't a modern spy movie; Elisha didn't have an electronic bug planted in the king of Syria's war room! But somehow, God was making known to Elisha what the king's plans were. And the king wasn't happy. So he did what you might expect in a modern spy movie: He sent a hit squad to find and capture the prophet.

The Lord Protects Us in Unseen Ways

God's ways are at times unusual and they are also, at times, unseen. That was true in this case. The king's officials learned that Elisha was in Dothan, so the king sent a "great army"—horses and chariots and soldiers—to capture one solitary prophet (2 Kings 6:13-14). So they surrounded the city at night in hopes of preventing Elisha's escape under the cover of darkness.

But Elisha didn't flee. The next morning, Elisha's servant went out and discovered the Syrian army surrounding them. He returned to Elisha with a predictable question: "Alas, my master! What shall we do?" (verse 15) All of us have asked that question innumerable times in our lives, haven't we? We need Elisha's perspective: "Do not fear, for those who are with us are more than those who are with them" (verse 16).

This whole story is filled with humorous moments. The servant and Elisha are two; the Syrian army is hundreds, at least. And yet Elisha says, "Don't worry; we have more than they do. Our army is bigger than their army." But then Elisha did what we need to do: He prayed. "Lord, I pray, open [my servant's] eyes that he may see" (verse 17). And God answered Elisha's prayer on the spot. Suddenly, the servant was able to see "the mountain was full of horses and chariots of fire all around Elisha" (verse 17). This was the angelic army of the Lord, normally invisible to humans. It's not that they became visible in this case. Rather, the servant was allowed to see into the spiritual realm and see the spiritual army of God filling the hills around the city.

I'm asked frequently if I believe we all have a guardian angel. I don't see evidence of that in Scripture, but I do see Hebrews 1:14 that says angels are spirit-servants sent to minister to those who will inherit salvation—meaning all who belong to God. God sent an army of those ministering spirits to protect Elisha and his servant that day.

Psalm 34:7 says, "The angel of the Lord encamps all around those who fear Him."

Psalm 91:11 says, "He shall give His angels charge over you, to keep you in all your ways."

This was not unusual in the Old Testament:

- Hagar was comforted by an angel.
- Abraham was visited by angels.
- Jacob wrestled all night with an angel.
- The Israelites were led by an angel through the desert.
- Gideon was instructed by an angel.
- David was disciplined by an angel.
- Elijah was fed by an angel.

And they were equally present in the New Testament:

- They announced Jesus' birth to Mary, to Joseph, and to the shepherds.

- They comforted Jesus when He was tempted by Satan in the wilderness.
- They strengthened Jesus in the Garden of Gethsemane.
- They gathered in hushed amazement before the cross and waited should He have beckoned them to rescue Him.
- They announced His resurrection.

Those are just a few examples of the manifestation of angels in the biblical stories. When we read these stories of angels, our first question is, do angels work the same way today? I firmly believe they do on the basis of Hebrews 1:14. In the same visible way as in the biblical stories? It seems not always, but that doesn't mean they aren't active in protecting us.

The history of world missionary activity is replete with accounts of angels protecting missionaries from people who were set to attack them and rid the land of the Gospel. But they would be repelled by large, fiery beings standing guard over the missionary compounds—unseen by the missionaries, but visible to the attackers. These sightings have tended to take place in spiritually dark regions of the world where spiritual warfare is the darkest. In our case, perhaps God withholds the sight of angels from us so we will not focus on them when our need is to focus on God alone. But I have no doubt that angels accompany us through our trials and give us comfort and protection.

As modern societies plunge deeper into spiritual darkness and nations abandon their Christian roots and biblical foundations, perhaps we will see an uptick of the presence and activity of angels as God's fiery armies come to stem the tide of evil in our world and protect the people of God.

The Lord Protects Us in Unexpected Ways

Now we see how God protected Elisha in an unexpected way —and can protect us in unexpected ways as well.

The Syrian army, unaware of the army of the Lord surrounding them, advanced towards Elisha's house. And Elisha prayed again: "Strike this people, I pray, with blindness" (2 Kings 6:18). And God answered this prayer as well—and the humor in this story continues.

Elisha went toward the blind Syrian army and told them—remember, they wouldn't have known who was talking to them—that Elisha was not there. But if they would follow him, he would lead them to where Elisha was staying. So, he led the Syrian army ten miles down the road to Samaria, the capital of Israel, and delivered them into the hands of Israel's army.

And Elisha prayed a third time: "Lord, open the eyes of these men, that they may see"—and He did (verse 20). When the Syrian soldiers opened their eyes, they were in Samaria! The army came to Dothan to get Elisha, but they wound up delivering themselves into the hands of the Israelite army. Instead of Elisha being taken prisoner, the Syrian army was taken prisoner by Israel.

So the king of Israel asked Elisha, "Shall I kill them?" (verse 21) And Elisha said "No." He told the king to set food and drink before them so they might eat and be refreshed and then return to their king in Syria. So the king of Israel did as Elisha said. The Syrians feasted in Samaria and then returned to Syria. "So the bands of Syrian raiders came no more into the land of Israel" (verse 23)—the perfect outcome for everyone.

It was Solomon who recommended giving your enemy food and drink; in doing so you may bring about his repentance (Proverbs 25:21-22). Paul quoted those proverbs in Romans 12:20 as a way to overcome evil with good. Such an act is not easy; it requires the love of God and the power of the Holy Spirit. But Elisha did it, and so must we.

Conclusion

This miracle story leaves us with two lessons for our own lives.

The Power of Perspective

We see the power of perspective when Elisha calmed the fears of his servant. The servant's perspective was that he and Elisha were surrounded by the Syrian army—and they were. But Elisha gave him a different perspective: "Those who are with us are more than those who are with them" (2 Kings 6:16). Elisha commanded the young man not to be afraid and then explained to him why. He gave his servant a different perspective on their problem. It's one thing to say, "Do not fear." It's another thing to say, "Do not fear because. . . ."

A change in perspective can change the outcome in a situation. Perspective can transform our fears into faith, our caution into courage. When we try to live our lives with only the perspective of the natural man—like the servant seeing the Syrian army with his natural eyes—then fear might be a reasonable response. But when we look at the situation through God's eyes, through a biblical lens, it can change everything.

What if, when we are faced with a threat or a problem, we could see the situation with faith-filled eyes? What if we could see the armies of heaven standing watch over our nation? What if we could see a band of angels standing guard over our home, our family, our children, our church? Things might be in turmoil in the natural world, but in the spiritual realm we would see God watching over His children.

It's worth noting that the servant's fear didn't go away until Elisha gave him a new perspective—until Elisha showed him the angels of God standing watch over them. That's how powerful perspective is. If we can see the unseen, if we can remember that "He who is in [us] is greater than he who is in the world" (1 John 4:4), we can have a new perspective as well.

The Possibilities of Prayer

Changing perspective is powerful, but when perspective is linked with prayer, new possibilities open up in front of us.

Three times in this story, Elisha prayed. First, that God would open the eyes of his servant that he might see things as they really are, not as they appear in the natural realm (2 Kings 6:17). Second, that God would close the eyes of those who meant to do them harm, the Syrian army (2 Kings 6:18). (This is basically what Corrie ten Boom prayed when she was being searched by the Nazi soldiers.) Third, he prayed that God would open the eyes of those same people, the Syrian soldiers, so they could see they were now powerless to carry out their hurtful mission (2 Kings 6:20).

Elisha lived in fulfillment of 1 Thessalonians 5:17, "Pray without ceasing." That doesn't mean walking around praying every second; it means living in a continuing conversation with God about your life. Problem comes up? Pray. Situations change? Pray. A need arises? Pray. A need met? Praise. I think the possibilities of prayer, living in continual dialogue with God, are beyond our wildest expectations.

Jesus' words in Mark 11:23-24 are worth noting as we close this lesson: "Whoever says to this mountain, 'Be removed and be cast into the sea,' and does not doubt in his heart, but believes that those things he says will be done, he will have whatever he says. Therefore I say to you, whatever things you ask when you pray, believe that you receive them, and you will have them."

May we not forget that the God who is living in us is greater than the god of this world. May we not forget that we can come into our God's presence in prayer any time we have a need. May we not forget that our perspective needs to be His perspective. May we not forget that coupling prayer with His perspective has the power to change everything (including us!).

Don't be guilty of saying, "I've tried everything else; there's nothing left to do now but pray." Instead, pray before you do anything else! And then look to see, with God's eyes, how things begin to change.

PERSONAL QUESTIONS

1. How do you reconcile the verses cited in this lesson about God's protection with the fact that sometimes bad things happen to Christians? (Psalm 27:1; Zechariah 9:15; John 17:11; 1 Peter 1:5)

2. Elisha knew what the Syrian army's plans were, yet he didn't flee from Dothan. Why not? What is the balance between faith and precaution in life?

3. What do you glean from the discussion about angels in this lesson?

   a. In what ways do you acknowledge the presence of angels in your daily life?

   b. What do verses like Hebrews 1:14 and 13:2 mean to you personally?

   c. Do you live with a supernatural perspective daily, aware of things happening in unseen realms? How might that help you live more courageously?

4. Read Daniel 10:1–11:1.
   a. For what was Daniel seeking understanding? (verse 1)

   b. How long did he pray and fast for understanding? (verse 2)

   c. When did the angel leave heaven to answer Daniel's prayer? (verse 12)

   d. What delayed the angel in arriving? (verse 13)

   e. What does this event tell you about supernatural activity unseen by man?

5. Does prayer feed perspective, or does perspective feed prayer? Or is it a cycle, one feeding the other? Explain how you understand the dynamics in this story.

6. Describe any personal experience in your life in which you think an angel might have been involved (or in the life of a friend).

GROUP QUESTIONS

1. Share your understanding of how to apply 1 Thessalonians 5:17 to the lives of busy people.

   a. What role does prayer play in your life? When and how do you pray?

   b. How do you see Elisha carrying out the principle of praying without ceasing as the miracles in this story unfolded?

   c. How would you distinguish between times of formal praying and informal praying?

   d. How do you feel about praying while driving, cooking, exercising, or doing other activities? If you would converse with a person during those activities, is it okay to converse with God?

   e. In what ways do we think of certain kinds of prayer as a conversation with God? What two things are part of any conversation? Speaking and____________________.

   f. How do you listen to God in prayer? How do you discern what He is communicating to you?

g. How often do you stop and pray with others about their simple needs? What results have you seen?

2. How do you feel about Elisha's decision not to harm his enemies, but to feed them? Could you have done what he did?

   a. Have you ever done anything similar—shower love upon someone who was your "enemy"?

   b. Why is love a better stimulant for repentance than vengeance?

DID YOU KNOW?

The admonition to love our enemies by giving them food and drink suggests an unusual result that such loving actions bring: "In doing this, you will heap burning coals on his head" (Proverbs 25:21-22, NIV). What does that odd expression mean? It likely has a cultural background since it is offered without explanation, as if the meaning is well known. There is a reference to burning coals falling on one's enemies in Psalm 140:10 as a form of retribution, but that seems contradictory to loving one's enemies. More likely, it may have an ancient Egyptian background: Guilty persons, as a sign of repentance, would carry a basin of hot coals on their heads. The suggestion in Proverbs is that being loving toward an enemy may stimulate repentance for his evil deeds.

A Day of Good News

2 Kings 6:24–7:20

In this lesson we see how God miraculously delivered on a promise that saved a city.

OUTLINE

People respond to good news differently. Some are skeptical and deny that it could be true; others doubt but are willing to consider it. When Elisha promised that God would meet the needs of a city, the responses were varied. Just as when people hear the Good News of the Gospel.

I. **The Promise of Good News**

II. **The People of Good News**

III. **The Proclamation of Good News**

IV. **The Proof of Good News**

V. **The Perfection of Good News**

VI. **Conclusion**
   A. Share the Good News in Your Life
   B. Share the Best News in Your Life

OVERVIEW

During the COVID–19 pandemic that occupied the world's attention in 2020–2021, there was a lot of bad news. There were deaths and illnesses, lost jobs, quarantines, and a downturn in the economy. But there was also good news: People using technology to reach out and communicate with friends and family they couldn't see in person, there was a boost in entrepreneurial activity as people found ways to generate income in a different environment, there was a new appreciation for frontline healthcare workers, and, of course, there was the rapid development of vaccines to arrest the spread of the virus.

Human beings long for good news! They will often find a way to generate it when bad news seems to be ruling the day. God has given us a resilient spirit, we crave good news.

Good News is, of course, the theme of the redemption story. The very word we use to define the Christian message of salvation —"Gospel"—is the word for "good news" in the original language of the New Testament. That word is found almost 100 times in the New Testament, in 19 of the 27 New Testament books.

Good News, the Gospel, was the central theme of the Lord Jesus Christ. When the angels announced His birth, they called it good news (Luke 1:19). When Jesus began His ministry, He went from town to town proclaiming good news (Matthew 4:23). And when He preached, He told people to repent and believe the Gospel (Mark 1:15). When He summarized His calling from God in a synagogue in Nazareth, by quoting from Isaiah 61:1-2, He included preaching the Gospel to the poor (Luke 4:18-19).

When the apostle Paul defined the Gospel in 1 Corinthians 15:1-4, he included what made it Good News: that we are saved by believing that Christ died for our sins and was resurrected. The opportunity to be saved from the penalty and power of sin and to be declared righteous in the sight of God is definitely Good News.

The story from the life of Elisha that we examine in this lesson is all about good news. Elisha promises it, four lepers proclaim it, the king of Israel doubts it, his servants prove it, and a messenger rejects it. That's like the Good News of the Gospel of Jesus Christ. Those who receive it are changed by it, but others doubt it and reject it. Not everyone is ready for Good News at the same time.

We have moved past the story of the king of Syria discussed in the previous lesson. There is a new king in Syria, Ben-Hadad. This king brings his army against Samaria, the capital of the ten northern tribes of Israel, and lays siege to it. This means there was no food coming in or out of the city during the siege and the people of Samaria were near starvation. They ultimately resorted to cannibalism, with mothers eating their own children (2 Kings 6:28-29). This is the terrible backdrop against which Elisha's next miracle takes place.

The Promise of Good News

The king of Israel, for some unknown reason, considered Elisha responsible for the famine in Samaria and thus the terrible condition of the people (2 Kings 6:31). The king sent a messenger to Elisha threatening to kill him if he didn't use his power to provide relief for the people of Samaria.

In response to the messenger, Elisha makes an unbelievable promise: Within a day, there will be plenty of flour and barley for sale in the city. The prices Elisha quoted were more than normal, but they represented a tremendous improvement over the situation as it existed (2 Kings 7:1). How would this happen? The messenger didn't believe it. The city was besieged by the army of Syria; people were resorting to eating any scrap of flesh and food they could find. Who could fault the king of Israel for doubting?

The king of Israel's messenger said, "Look, if the Lord would make windows in heaven, could this thing be?" (verse 2) Because of the messenger not believing God would provide, Elisha told him he would eat none of the food when God provided it. Elisha didn't take kindly to the messenger mocking and doubting God. When good news is given, people who are starving ought to embrace that news. There is a price to pay, temporally and eternally, for rejecting God's Good News and provision.

Let's be honest—lots of people are inclined to embrace bad news before embracing good news. Even when Christians get together to catch up with one another, often bad news will dominate the conversation. Why is that? We have the best news the world has ever known, yet too often we focus on the bad news instead of the Good News. Spreading bad news doesn't do anybody any good. Instead, we should be spreading the Good News, encouraging one another with the truth about God's goodness.

When I was a young pastor in my first church, trying to build a new church in a new community, I was invited to a local pastors' prayer meeting. I went a few times, then stopped attending. I felt worse after attending because there was so much sharing of bad news among the pastors—about their churches, their finances, their members. I decided it wasn't helping me to get a weekly dose of bad news, so I stopped attending.

As we went about building that new church from the ground up, there were plenty of things that qualified as bad news. And I found myself dwelling on those until the Lord showed me one day: If I just looked, I could find some good news to focus on every day. And that's what I began to do and have tried to do ever since. There is always something to rejoice over when you know Jesus Christ. I've always been grateful to have learned that lesson early in my pastoral ministry. As Christians, we need to be focused on the Good News that accompanies the Gospel!

The People of Good News

The story continues but the scene shifts to the city of Samaria. Sitting outside the gate of the city were four lepers. They weren't allowed inside the city because of their leprosy, yet surrounding the city was the Syrian army. They were trapped in a sort of no-man's land. So they talked about what they should do (2 Kings 7:3-4). They had two choices: stay outside the gates of the city where they would starve or throw themselves on the mercy of the Syrian army who might give them something to eat.

They decided the second option was preferable, so they set out at twilight for the camp of the Syrian army. And there they discovered something amazing. When they arrived at the outskirts of the army's camp, there was no one there. There was not a single soldier to be seen, yet all their equipment and horses and donkeys were still there. It was as if they had picked up and marched off in a sudden panic. The Syrian soldiers had heard, in the dark, the sound of an approaching army. They thought the king of Israel had hired Hittites and Egyptians as mercenaries to fight against them. So they fled their camp (verses 5-7)!

Actually, it was a "miracle of noise." The Lord caused the Syrian army to hear the noise that would have been generated by a massive approaching army—but there was no army. They heard voices, horses, chariot wheels on the gravel, trumpets blaring—

every noise that an advancing army would have generated. Rather than waiting to see who the army was, and possibly get into a battle they would probably lose, the Syrian army fled in the night leaving all their provisions behind. But again—there was no advancing army.

The lepers thought they had hit the jackpot! They had walked into a camp with enough food and provisions to feed an army. They went from tent to tent collecting silver, gold, clothing, and anything else of value. They carried the loot away and hid it and returned for more (verse 8). They went from desperation to deliverance, from bad news to good news, in a matter of a few short hours.

The Proclamation of Good News

But the lepers eventually had a "light bulb" moment; their consciences kicked in while they were collecting things just for themselves. They realized that what they had found should be shared with others (verses 9-11).

Then and now, good news is for sharing. They realized they couldn't keep the bounty to themselves in light of what was happening in the city of Samaria where people were starving. They couldn't even wait until morning; they decided to go to Samaria immediately and tell the king that the army had fled and left behind all their food and provisions (verse 9). They arrived at the city and conveyed the news to the city gatekeepers who spread the word inside the city.

These men were excited about their good fortune and they wanted to share it with others who were in need. That's the secret to evangelism—excitement! If we possess what we truly believe to be life-changing Good News, we can't keep it to ourselves. We have to share it with others.

The Proof of Good News

Sadly, not everyone welcomes good news as they should. When news of the bounty left by the Syrian army reached the king of Israel, he didn't believe it. He thought it was a trap. He thought the Syrians were hiding in the surrounding hills and forests waiting to attack the people of Samaria when they went out to loot the Syrian camp (verse 12). But he was willing to check it out. The messenger we met earlier, the one who doubted God would provide wheat and barley for the city, was a true skeptic. But we can call the king a seeker—he was willing to look for evidence that the Syrians had departed, leaving their food for the Israelites in Samaria.

So the king sent some men in two chariots out to assess the situation; they found it to be just as the lepers had described. The army was gone; all that was left was scattered equipment and clothing left behind as the Syrian army fled. So the men returned and reported to the king that the food and provisions of the Syrian army were theirs for the taking. So the people of Samaria rushed out of the city and plundered the Syrian army's camp (and trampled the skeptical messenger to death in the rush). Not only was the siege over, but so was the famine. Just as Elisha had prophesied, there was abundant barley and flour to be bought in the city (2 Kings 7:14-20).

The Perfection of Good News

Remember the original prophecy in 2 Kings 7:1? Within 24 hours, there would be choice flour and barley grain available to be bought in Samaria. Twenty-four hours later, there was choice flour and barley grain available to be bought in Samaria (verses 17-18). What seemed like an absolutely impossible promise came true just as the prophet Elisha said it would. When a promise is made, it *sounds* like good news. But when a promise is *kept*, it becomes, in fact, good news. Those who embrace the words of the Gospel and give their lives to Jesus discover that the promise of the Gospel is true.

Conclusion

We could draw many applications from this amazing miracle story involving Elisha, but I want to highlight two that focus on what to do with good news.

Share the Good News in Your Life

There could be many reasons we don't share the good news we have. If a person's having a bad day, they might resent us coming in all excited with our good news. But in fact, it's people who are having a bad day (or life) who are often the most receptive to good news. Our good news might be just the blessing they need. When you bless someone else by sharing the Good News about Jesus, and they receive the Gospel, it blesses you, too. It becomes a blessing for them and a blessing for you as well.

Sometimes we don't think we are worthy representatives of the Gospel, or we think we don't have anything profound to share. We forget that we don't have to be worthy of the Good News; that's part of the Gospel itself. Jesus came to save us because we are not worthy to save ourselves. And that is good news for us and for others who may not feel worthy to receive it. But there is always something God is doing in our life that is worth sharing with others.

If we are walking with the Lord daily, we can always encourage others with some aspect of the Gospel of grace. We can share something that God has done in our life that will encourage another person. We can share a small piece of the Bread of Life with a hungry soul—just enough that could make a difference in their life that day.

Share the Best News in Your Life

As Christians, the news we have to share is not just Good News; it is the best news anyone could possibly be given. Yes, the translation of the Greek word in the New Testament is "good news." I'm not changing the definition to "best news." But given what the Gospel says, and what it represents, it is the best news anyone could ever hope to hear. You might have a number of positive things to impart to a needy person you encounter, but the best thing you can say to them is that God loves them.

Sometimes Christians don't share the Gospel because they think they need to be trained or go to a class on witnessing. Classes and training are great; we should all avail ourselves of those resources. But a witness for Christ is the same as a witness in a courtroom. We tell what we have seen and heard. That's what the apostle John focused on when he wrote about Jesus (1 John 1:1, 3). That's all witnessing for Jesus is—telling what you have seen Jesus do in your own life. We don't have to have all the answers to all the questions. If we are telling what God has done in our life, no one can question that. That's all a witness does—says what he or she knows to be true.

Maybe you are reading these words and you realize you can't tell what Jesus has done for you because you have never begun a relationship with Him. I have good news for you! You can begin to know Him today by confessing your need for Him and believing that He died for your sins and rose to give you new life in Him. Do that and you'll have good news to share with others.

PERSONAL QUESTIONS

1. Read 2 Kings 7:9. To what degree can you identify with the lepers' attitude—feeling compelled to share the good news? How often do you share the Gospel with non-Christians?

   a. What is the primary obstacle you feel to sharing the Gospel?

   b. Why are Christians in general reticent to witness for Christ?

   c. Based on your Christian experience, what "benefits" of knowing Christ could you share with another person? (List the main benefits in your life of being a Christian.)

2. Based on Matthew 4:23 and 9:35, how central to Jesus' message was the Gospel?

   a. He hadn't been crucified and resurrected at this point, so what was the good news He was preaching?

   b. Are the Gospel of the kingdom and the Gospel of Christ's death and resurrection the same? How do they fit together?

3. Read Isaiah 61:1-2 and Luke 4:18-19. How did Jesus see Himself fulfilling the Messianic prophecy of Isaiah in terms of the Gospel?

a. Identify the kind of "good news" Jesus planned to preach to the following categories of people: (Luke 4:18-19)

- the poor

- the prisoners

- the blind

- the oppressed

- to all

b. In what way would these proclamations qualify as Jesus preaching the "gospel of the kingdom"?

4. When you first heard the Gospel of Jesus, were you a skeptic? A seeker? How long did it take you to embrace the Gospel?

GROUP QUESTIONS

1. See if your group can come up with an "elevator pitch" summary of the Christian Gospel: the facts of the Gospel in one brief sentence as an answer when someone asks you, "What is the Gospel?" (See 1 Corinthians 15:1-4.)

2. Share how you first heard the Gospel message: over time or in one presentation from a Christian friend, witness, or evangelist.

   a. What part of the "Good News" was the "best news" for you? What part of the Gospel touched you most deeply?

b. What experience have you had sharing the Gospel with others? How have you done it?

c. How does the definition of a witness (share what you have "seen and heard") take some of the fear out of witnessing? (1 John 1:1, 3)

3. In this lesson, the king's messenger was a skeptic, and the king himself was a seeker when it came to Elisha's promise of good news (2 Kings 7:2, 11-12). When sharing the Gospel, how should we respond to both of those types of people? (1 Peter 3:15-16)

a. Were you a skeptic or a seeker before you became a Christian, when you first heard the Gospel?

b. What positive or negative responses did the person sharing the Gospel have toward you?

c. How did their response help or hinder your own decision-making process?

DID YOU KNOW?

The unbelievable instance of two women making a pact to kill, cook, and eat their children during the siege of Samaria (2 Kings 6:26-29) was actually foretold in Leviticus and Deuteronomy. It was part of the curse that would come upon Israel if she abandoned the covenant obligations of the law. Breaking covenant with God would result in the nation being overtaken by her enemies, which would include sieges of her cities. Food would be cut off, and inhabitants would resort to killing and eating their own children. It is first mentioned to the Exodus generation in Leviticus 26:27-29, then reiterated and expanded to the conquest generation in Deuteronomy 28:53-57. Even the desperation of a woman hiding her child so she wouldn't have to share was foretold (2 Kings 6:29; Deuteronomy 28:56-57). It also happened during the siege of Jerusalem by Babylon (Lamentations 2:20; 4:9-10).

The Blessing of a Consistent Life

2 Kings 8:1-6

In this lesson we see what it means to live a consistent life while waiting on God.

OUTLINE

Life is a marathon, not a sprint. Those words apply to the Christian life as well. Consistency in anything requires one thing: time. Consistency is especially important in fallow times when waiting on God. This lesson is about a woman whose consistency was honored by God.

I. She Continued to Walk According to God's Word

II. She Continued to Wait on God's Plan

A. Waiting Results in Perception
B. Waiting Results in Protection
C. Waiting Results in Perspective
D. Waiting Results in Provision
E. Waiting Results in Power

III. She Continued to Witness About God's Grace

OVERVIEW

I recently read a helpful book by James Clear: *Atomic Habits: An Easy & Proven Way to Build Good Habits & Break Bad Ones*. His theme in the book is that little changes in our habits can result in big changes in our lives. He writes that we underrate the power of developing small, consistent habits. He says many people make the mistake of focusing on *intensity*, when what we should focus on is *consistency*.

Consistency: don't miss a scheduled workout for two years; write in your journal every week; practice daily silent meditation.

Intensity: Run a marathon; write a book in thirty days; go on a silent meditation retreat.

He says it's the simple, small things that you do over and over that make a difference in our life.

I believe this theme of consistency runs throughout the Bible. Look at the daily and yearly movement of the heavenly bodies, the regular replication of genetic codes over generations, and other manifestations of consistency in God's creation. Given God's consistency over time, how might we expect to grow spiritually? Consistently, over time, of course! We don't mature overnight; we don't put a Bible under our pillow one night and wake up mature the next morning.

The Christian life is a *daily* life. We have mountaintop experiences along the way, but we always have to come back to the valley where daily life is lived. We grow spiritually like the miner who digs and picks at the ground daily—consistently, expectantly —until he uncovers things of value. It is interesting that Solomon compared acquiring wisdom and understanding to mining for buried treasure (Proverbs 2:1-5). Daily, devoted progress yields results in the end. Even Jesus *"kept increasing* in wisdom and stature, and in favor with God and people" as a young man (Luke 2:52, NASB, emphasis added). God wants us to keep increasing daily as well.

In this lesson from the life of Elisha, we'll focus on the blessing of a consistent life. That's the kind of life God wants us to lead—not up and down, but steady and consistent, day after day as we follow Christ and the leading of the Spirit. The Bible uses the word "continue" as a way to speak of consistency.

Jesus admired the faithfulness of the crowds who "continued with [Him] three days" (Mark 8:2). The Early Church in Jerusalem "continued steadfastly in the apostles' doctrine and fellowship" (Acts 2:42). James says those are blessed who continue in God's Word (James 1:25). One of the most consistent people in the Bible was Daniel, who "continued until the first year of King Cyrus" in Babylon, then Persia (Daniel 1:21). Daniel was taken from Jerusalem to Babylon as a teenager and served as a prophet-in-exile for almost seventy years. He was faithful; he continued serving God; he was consistent in a godly life all those decades. Through all the intrigues and subterfuge of a pagan royal court, Daniel followed God without wavering in his consistency.

As the kings and leaders cycled through Mesopotamia, Daniel was unmoved; he stayed the course at all times. Leaders, circumstances, and situations changed, but Daniel remained true and consistent. There might be no better epitaph on one's tombstone at the end of life than "He continued."

With that background, we pick up the story of Elisha's ministry in Israel. And we go back to the story of the woman from Shunem in 2 Kings 4:8-37. She and her husband had constructed a guest room for Elisha to use when he visited Shunem. The woman and her husband had no children, but Elisha prophesied that they would have a son within the year, which they did. But when the son was small, he died, and the woman beseeched Elisha to help her. Elisha worked a miracle and the boy was restored to life—raised from the dead.

This woman appears again in Elisha's life a number of years later. In 2 Kings 8:1 we pick up her story.

She Continued to Walk According to God's Word

Elisha had apparently stayed in contact with the family over the years; in verse 1 we see him delivering a message, a warning, to her. Elisha tells her the Lord is going to send a famine on the land. She and her household should leave the area and find somewhere to live for the next seven years—the length of the famine. She took Elisha at his word, packing up her household and moving to the land of the Philistines for the next seven years (verse 2).

Verse 2 says she "did according to the saying of the man of God [Elisha]." There is no indication of debate or argument; she took Elisha's words for what they were—a clear warning from God.

And based on her history with Elisha as a prophet, it is no surprise that she "proceeded to do" (verse 2, NIV) what Elisha suggested. She accomplished all that Elisha said to do.

Walking according to God's Word is at the heart of a consistent Christian life. The apostle James warned his readers, "But be doers of the word, and not hearers only, deceiving yourselves" (James 1:22). He goes on to say that those who "do" the Word are those who will be blessed in what they do (verse 25). We come up with all kinds of activities that we hope will result in being blessed, and they might. But the Bible puts a premium on knowing and doing the Word of God. "Blessed is the man [whose] . . . delight is in the law of the Lord" (Psalm 1:1-2).

I've observed over the years that there is a gap in many Christians' experiences between what they read in the Bible and what they do in their daily life. The gap is between what we know and what we do. Many Christians have been in church most of their lives. They know a lot of the Bible but have settled into a routine of reading and hearing without feeling motivated or obligated to do it. We need to approach the Bible with a predetermined commitment to do what it says to do every time we read it.

I think the Shunammite woman had that perspective. Elisha gave her very brief instructions and she did exactly what he said. Moving to the land of the pagan Philistines was a step of faith. But she had seen God give her a son, then raise that son back to life. So she had experience with the provision of God through His prophet. That's the fruit of consistency in her life. The longer we walk with God, see Him work, and learn to trust Him, the more ready we are to obey Him when He tells us what to do—even if we don't totally understand or have all the information we would like.

She Continued to Wait on God's Plan

The woman and her household stayed in the land of the Philistines for seven years. At the end of the seven years, she returned to the land of Israel (2 Kings 8:3). We know nothing about their life in Philistia except that they were alive and well at the end of the seven years. So she waited and worked patiently, obeying what God had told her to do. We have to believe that God provided for her and protected her during her patient waiting period.

God doesn't call us to do something and send us out with a "Good luck!" wish. When He calls or directs, He is committed to providing what that call requires. Obeying Him, then watching Him provide, is one of the ways He teaches us and prepares us for continued obedience in the future. We do know she seemed to have the gift of service and hospitality, based on her family's ministry to Elisha. So God probably used her gifts to help her connect with people in Philistia and generate a network of support for those seven years. God always provides!

If you are waiting on God, don't wait passively, wait actively. Continue to move and serve while you are waiting. My experience has been that it is in the process of obedient service that God continues to unfold His plans and will for our life. As the saying goes, it's hard to steer a car or a battleship that isn't moving. It is the same with us. God can steer us much more easily if we are already in motion for Him.

I know of at least five good things that happen when we wait actively on the Lord.

Waiting Results in Perception

The psalmist wrote, "Show me Your ways, O Lord; teach me Your paths. . . . on You I wait all the day" (Psalm 25:4-5). Most people in our society don't like to wait; I am one of them. I want God to show me what to do yesterday! But sometimes God calls us to wait. And while we are waiting, we increase in perception.

Waiting Results in Protection

When we wait, we slow down and don't move as fast—and that may be one of the ways God protects us from getting into something that could be harmful or detrimental. The psalmist wrote, "Our soul waits for the Lord; He is our help and our shield" (Psalm 33:20). In a world in which only God can see the future, we need to trust that His leading to wait may be for our own protection and best interests.

Waiting Results in Perspective

Psalm 37:7 says, "Rest in the Lord, and wait patiently for Him; do not fret because of him who prospers in his way, because of the man who brings wicked schemes to pass." When we look around us, it seems like the bad people prosper; it seems they get away with things that others don't. You are trying to be faithful to God and you don't end up as seemingly prosperous as those who don't care about God. But God says, "Wait." Don't try to fix things; don't try to be like others; don't try to take matters into your own hands. Wait on the Lord to show Himself strong on your behalf. Let Him give you a different perspective. An entire psalm, Psalm 73, chronicles the psalmist's wrestling with this issue and how his perspective changed.

Waiting Results in Provision

"The Lord is good to those who wait for Him, to the soul who seeks Him. It is good that one should hope and wait quietly for the salvation of the Lord" (Lamentations 3:25-26). Sometimes we may be out of work, out of options, out of hope or patience, or even out of money. And we wonder where God is in the midst of our need. The Bible says that God is good to those who wait on Him and seek Him. In fact, it says that "it is good" to wait and hope. God never abandons His children when they are waiting on Him.

Waiting Results in Power

Finally, waiting results in new power: "Those who wait on the Lord shall renew their strength" (Isaiah 40:31). Sometimes when we are weak—physically, spiritually, relationally—a time of waiting is exactly what we need to renew and restore our strength. Sometimes it takes a time of isolation or seclusion to rebuild our strength and vigor in order to come back into the stream of life. We always come out stronger in those times than when we went in.

"Trust" is another way of saying "wait." When we wait on the Lord, we have to trust Him until the time of waiting is over. The Shunammite woman waited and trusted the Lord for seven years.

She Continued to Witness About God's Grace

It's amazing how "coincidences" seem to happen in the lives of those who wait and trust the Lord. When the Shunammite woman returned to Israel, she wanted to get her home and property restored to her. So she went to see the king of Israel (2 Kings 8:3-6). It just so happened that at the exact moment she entered the king's presence, Gehazi, Elisha's servant, was in a conversation with the king. The king had asked Gehazi to tell him about the things Elisha had done, and Gehazi mentioned Elisha having brought the dead back to life.

Gehazi looked up and saw the woman from Shunem, whose son Elisha had brought back to life, and he said, "My lord, O king, this is the woman, and this is her son whom Elisha restored to life" (verse 5). What a "coincidence"! The king asked the woman to tell him what Elisha had done for her, and she did. She testified to the king about the power and grace of God delivered through His prophet, Elisha.

She was in the same position many of us are at various times in our lives. She had moved away from her home for seven years. She approaches an unknown future. Will she get her property back? Will she have a place for she and her son to live? What will happen? All she knew to do was to do "the next right thing." She gave a testimony of how God had raised her son from the dead, how Elisha's warning about the famine had saved their lives, and how she was now back seeking to rebuild her life in the land of Israel. In other words, she didn't have answers to all her questions, but she gave testimony to what she did know: God is good; I trust Him.

When things on the horizon look fuzzy and unclear, what are we to do? We simply do what we have always done if we are being consistent. We trust, we give God praise for His goodness, and we wait on Him to reveal His will for our next steps. It's not our job to figure out what God is doing or figure out what we should do. Our job is to actively trust Him through prayer, counsel, studying His Word, serving (so He can move us as we are moving), and worshiping Him. We live faithfully, doing what we know to do.

Sometimes when I'm waiting on a big decision, or waiting on the outcome of an election, someone will ask, "What are you going to do if the outcome isn't what you expect?" My answer is, "I'm going to do what I always do: pray, study, preach, teach, pastor the church, do radio and television. I'm going to do what I've always done until God says to do something different."

That's what the Shunammite woman did. And guess what the king did? He restored her house and property to her and seven years' worth of income that she lost because of the famine (verse 6). She waited; she prayed; she was faithful and consistent—and God honored her for it. I believe He wants to do the same for us—for all who live consistently before Him.

PERSONAL QUESTIONS

1. Read Proverbs 2:1-5.

   a. What do you learn about conditions from the three "if's" (verses 1, 3, 4) and the "then" word? (verse 5) Why is spiritual maturity conditional rather than unconditional?

   b. What are the three conditions?

      Verse 1:

      Verse 3:

      Verse 4:

   c. What is the result if the conditions are met? (verse 5)

d. In general, what daily spiritual activity for a Christian is described in . . .

Verse 1:

Verse 2:

Verse 3:

Verse 4:

e. Considering verse 4: How many prospectors strike it rich in a single day? How are most nuggets extracted from the ground in prospecting (at least in ancient times)?

f. What does that say about how we find "the fear of the Lord" and "the knowledge of God"? (verse 5)

2. How long have you been a Christian?

   a. On a scale of 1 to 10 (10 = very consistent), how consistent have your spiritual disciplines and practices been?

   b. In what way does your spiritual maturity match/not match your consistency?

   c. What area of your spiritual life would benefit most from more consistency?

   d. How easy have you found it to be inconsistent? How much accountability do you have from fellow believers? (e.g., a small group)

GROUP QUESTIONS

1. Share your perceptions of spiritual consistency overall. Steady progress toward maturity? Erratic ups and downs?

   a. What are the most consistent aspects of your spiritual life? (e.g., study, prayer, etc.)

   b. What are the most inconsistent aspects of your spiritual life?

   c. What are the biggest obstacles to greater consistency? What would help remove those obstacles?

   d. To whom are you accountable in your Christian life? Who knows what's happening in your life "behind the scenes"?

2. Share about "waiting periods" in your life (past or present). What were you waiting for? (e.g., answer to prayer, direction, calling, etc.)

   a. How long did the waiting period last? What was your spiritual "demeanor" during that period?

   b. How did the waiting period end? Suddenly? Gradually?

   c. What did you learn? How did you grow?

3. Does Luke 2:52 surprise you, that Jesus had to "grow" in maturity?

   a. What does it say about growth over time that His ministry only began in His early thirties?

   b. Are you satisfied with where you are spiritually in terms of knowledge, service, or maturity?

   c. Think of Christians you know and admire in terms of maturity, service, and relationships. To what do you attribute their consistency in their spiritual walk?

DID YOU KNOW?

The Shunammite woman had to leave Israel because of a famine, a tool used by God to remind His people that they were living outside their covenant obligations to Him. When Solomon dedicated the temple to God, he prayed that when the people broke God's commands and experienced a famine, that He would forgive them when they repented, that He would remove the famine (1 Kings 8:35-40). The people shouldn't have missed the warning sign of famines—they were clearly specified in the list of curses for breaking God's covenant (Leviticus 26:18-20; Deuteronomy 28:18, 23-24). In the text of this story about the Shunammite woman, there is no indication as to why the famine ended. Possibly because of King Jehu's campaign against Baal worship in Israel (2 Kings 10:18-28).

Elisha's Final Miracle

2 Kings 13:14-21

In this lesson we learn about deliverance and devotion through Elisha's final miracle.

OUTLINE

Elisha lived until approximately the age of ninety after serving as a prophet of God in Israel for a half-century. Even near his death—even after his death—the prophetic power of God continued to be manifest. In this concluding lesson we draw lessons that speak to our eternal destiny.

I. **Elisha's Final Message**
   A. The Promise of Deliverance
   B. The Principle of Devotion

II. **Elisha's Final Miracle**

III. **Conclusion**
   A. A Word About Deliverance
   B. A Word About Devotion
   C. A Word About Destiny

OVERVIEW

Dr. James Dobson made some observations about growing old that are well worth noting. "The world seems to worship youth and is terrified of aging. But there was a time when getting older was associated with wisdom and experience. In fact, some of the greatest accomplishments in history came very late in life. Immanuel Kant wrote one of his best philosophical works at the age of seventy-four. Verdi penned his classic 'Ave Maria' at eighty-five. Michelangelo was eighty-seven when he completed *The Pietá*, his greatest work of art. Justice Oliver Wendell Holmes set down some of his most brilliant opinions at the age of ninety. And Ronald Reagan was the most powerful man in the world at seventy-five. This notion that life should be winding down at fifty or sixty years of age is crazy."[1]

I believe the prophet, Elisha, would agree with those words. As we close our study of Elisha, we will find him growing old but still serving the Lord. At this point in his life, he is at least ninety years old, having served God and Israel as a prophet for at least half a century. In this closing look at Elisha's life and ministry, we find him delivering a final message and a final miracle.

Elisha's Final Message

In 2 Kings 13:14, we discover that "Elisha had become sick with the illness of which he would die." Joash, king of Israel, was distraught over Elisha's illness and imminent death, and went to visit him, weeping over him.

In 2 Kings 13, we find Israel at one of the lowest points in her history. As a result of being ruled by a series of evil kings, the Syrians routinely attacked and defeated them. Israel is down to "fifty horsemen, ten chariots, and ten thousand foot soldiers" (2 Kings 13:7). Joash, the king, had done evil in the sight of the Lord and enjoyed no blessings from God on his reign or the nation (2 Kings 13:10-11).

In spite of his wickedness, Joash wept when he learned Elisha was about to die. Was he truly sad at losing God's prophet, or was he sad at losing someone who might be able to help his crippled nation? We don't know. Regardless, Elisha responds to Joash's sorrow with a message of hope.

The Promise of Deliverance

Elisha had Joash act out a mini-drama to illustrate what God was prepared to do for the nation. Elisha told Joash to take a bow and some arrows; he told Joash to hold the bow, then he put his hand on top of Joash's hand on the bow. He had Joash shoot an arrow out of the east window of the room, saying the arrow represented the arrow of God's deliverance from Syria if they would attack Syria at Aphek (2 Kings 13:15-17).

There was the promise; God was prepared to deliver Israel from the Syrian army. It was a certain promise from God through His prophet. This promise had nothing to do with strength. Elisha was ninety years old; the king was wicked and unrighteous; Israel was down to a meager fighting force. It was based solely on the grace and strength of the Lord.

"Deliverance" is a powerful theme in Scripture, occurring more than five hundred times. Jesus delivered us from our sins (Galatians 1:3-4). He has delivered us from the power of darkness (Colossians 1:13). He delivers us from the wrath to come (1 Thessalonians 1:10). And He is able to deliver us from temptation (2 Peter 2:9). Deliverance by the strength of the Lord comes in all different forms. Just as God stood ready to deliver Israel from Syria, He stands ready to deliver you and me from any snare or temptation.

The Principle of Devotion

As we have seen many times already, prophets do things that folks who are not prophets would never think to do. And Elisha now does something unusual. He promised Joash deliverance but found the king's devotion lacking. Elisha tied Joash's (Israel's) deliverance to the intensity of Joash's devotion—and found the latter wanting.

After Joash shot the arrow, Elisha told him to take some arrows and strike the ground with them; Joash struck the ground three times. And Elisha reacted angrily, telling him he should have struck the ground five or six times. Because he only struck the ground three times, Joash would not defeat Syria totally but only strike the Syrian army three times (2 Kings 13:18-19).

Elisha was testing Joash. He wanted Joash to strike the ground repeatedly with the arrows to demonstrate his total devotion and commitment to what God was promising to do for him. But the king only struck the ground three times, a half-hearted response, at best.

As one commentator put it, "[Joash] was content with only three victories.... God gave him a blank check, but he only cashed half of it. The king missed his golden opportunity."[2]

Sometimes we do the same thing in our Christian life—avail ourselves of only part of what God wants to do in and for us. We must be fully devoted to Christ in every aspect of our life. Whatever we do, as Paul wrote, we must "do it heartily, as to the Lord and not to men" (Colossians 3:23).

In verse 25, we learn what happened. Joash defeated Ben-Hadad, the Syrian king, three times, just as Elisha predicted. That's better than not defeating him at all. But he could have been even more victorious. He got as many victories as his devotion indicated he would; he got as many victories as he trusted God for.

Elisha's final message was about deliverance and devotion, the relationship between the two. May our devotion be such that we are serious when it comes to asking God for deliverance from the troubles in our life.

Elisha's Final Miracle

If firing arrows and striking arrows seemed unusual, Elisha's final "miracle" sets the bar even higher for prophetic practice.

Elisha died and was buried (2 Kings 13:20). At that time, groups of Moabite raiders used to launch raids throughout Israel to plunder where they could. One day, when some Israelites were burying a man who had died, they spied a band of Moabite raiders approaching. So they tossed the dead man's body into Elisha's tomb and ran for their lives. As soon as the man's body touched Elisha's bones, the dead man came back to life (verse 21)!

Elisha had raised the dead while he was living (the Shunammite woman's young son), but now he raises someone from the dead while he himself is dead! Elisha continues to be a source of life even after he is physically dead. What a story and what a thought! We may not be able to duplicate Elisha's miracle, but we can certainly influence the lives of others after we are gone. Our words and our actions outlive us. We can be a source of life and encouragement to others by the legacy we create and leave behind when we've gone to heaven.

My parents gave me a copy of the *Scofield Reference Bible* for my sixteenth birthday. I read it constantly, especially the notes Scofield had penned. And one day I noticed that the date of original publication was 1909, and I was reading it in the 1950s. So decades after his study Bible was produced, and Scofield was with the Lord, the crowning achievement of his walk with the Lord was still influencing Christians like me—and it is still being consulted more than a century later! All of us can have some kind of impact like that. Maybe not through writing or publishing, but through the children and grandchildren we influence, through the missionaries we support, through the churches we help to grow. We don't do it for praise, or just to be remembered. We do the work now as a service to the Kingdom of God, and if it is fruit that is good, then that fruit will remain long after we are gone (John 15:5, 16).

Conclusion

Here are three lessons we can draw and apply to our lives from Elisha's final message and miracle.

A Word About Deliverance

Elisha spoke a word of deliverance to a sinful, wicked king who was responsible for the suffering of his entire nation by the covenant curses of the law. Elisha's message was one of pure grace. What God did for Joash reminds us of what God has done for us: "But God demonstrates His own love toward us, in that while we were still sinners, Christ died for us" (Romans 5:8).

Paul wrote those words after giving an illustration: It's possible that someone might consent to die as a substitute for a good person, more so for an exceptionally good person. But who would die for an evil person, a criminal who lived a life of sin? And yet that's what Christ did for us: "While we were still sinners, Christ died for us." We weren't good people; we certainly weren't exceptional people. We were sinners; we were enemies of God (Romans 5:10). In spite of who we were, Christ died for us. That is pure grace.

Paul paints a picture of who humanity was and is in Romans 3:9-18—and it is not a pretty picture. But his words illustrate the grace of God. In spite of our sin and lack of even caring for God, Christ died for us.

And in spite of Joash being one of Israel's most wicked kings, Elisha spoke a promise of deliverance to him. It could have been more if Joash's heart had been in it. But the partial victory Israel experienced was more than Joash deserved. That's what deliverance by grace is all about.

A Word About Devotion

Joash failed to go "all in" on the promise Elisha gave him about deliverance from the Syrians. I citied Colossians 3:23 earlier—a verse about going all in for God based on His ability to work powerfully on our behalf. Another verse that says something similar is 1 Corinthians 15:58: "Be steadfast, immovable, always abounding in the work of the Lord, knowing that your labor is not in vain in the Lord." And Colossians 3:17 says, "Whatever you do in word or deed, do all in the name of the Lord Jesus." One more: "Therefore, whether you eat or drink, or whatever you do, do all to the glory of God" (1 Corinthians 10:31).

These verses speak to the whole issue of having a devoted heart, having a heart full of devotion to God. At the beginning of the day, we should rise committed and devoted to God's work. At the end of the day, we should retire knowing we left nothing undone. We should be tired at the end of the day, but when it is a godly kind of tired, from serving God with our gifts and the power He provides, we can sleep well.

Mike Nappa catches the heart of a life devoted to God: "I've got news for you. True Christianity, courageous Christianity—the kind the apostles Paul and Peter and thousands of other early Christians practiced—isn't for wimps. It's not for the fainthearted, the lukewarm, the moderately committed, or the occasional churchgoer. It's for the passionate, the ones with the courage to say, 'I believe God, and I will dedicate my every waking hour to his purpose, no matter what it costs.'"[3]

God used Joash a little; He could have used him a lot. If we want to be used by God to the extent of our abilities, we have to be all in when it comes to devotion.

A Word About Destiny

A man was surprisingly resurrected from the dead when he came in contact with Elisha's bones. But the Bible promises a resurrection that will be no surprise when it happens: the resurrection to eternal life of those who have put their faith in Christ.

When United States Supreme Court Justice Lewis Powell, IV died in 1998 at the age of ninety, pastor and scholar James C. Goodloe spoke these words of hope at his funeral: "We rejoice in Christ's resurrection as the promise of our own as the promise of resurrection of those whom we love.... Death pretends to be Lord over us. It's not. God alone is the Lord over our lives. Death tries to have the last word about who we are. It doesn't. God has plans for our lives that even death cannot destroy. Death struts its seeming great power, but its power is broken. To Christ belongs the victory. Though death will lay claim to all of us, it will not hold us all, for we do not belong to death. We belong to God in life, we belong to God in death, and we continue to belong to God in that new life on the other side of death."[4]

The man who was revived when he touched Elisha's bones was an Old Testament glimpse of the New Testament truth: Death is not final. God is Lord over death. God is Lord over life, death, and eternal life. Some people spend their whole lives fearing death (Hebrews 2:15). They live in fear of death, and they die in fear of death. But not the Christian—because Christ conquered death at His own resurrection (1 Corinthians 15:54-57). What was only glimpsed in the Old Testament was fully revealed in the New.

Every human being must ask himself or herself at some point, *What is my destiny? Am I prepared for my life on this earth to end?* The man coming back to life in the presence of Elisha's bones was a one-off event. For the rest of us, "It is appointed for men to die once, but after this the judgment" (Hebrews 9:27).

How would you answer those questions about your destiny? If you stand before God after you die and He asks, "Why should I let you into My heaven?" … what would you say? Your answer can have nothing to do with being a good person or doing good works. For we have all sinned and fallen short of God's standard (Romans 3:23). We can be saved only by the grace of God through faith in Christ (Ephesians 2:8-9). That is the only answer that can make you certain of your eternal destiny.

As powerful as the miracles of Elisha were, they pale in comparison to the miracle God wants to do in your heart today: Give you a new life, now and for all eternity.

Notes

1. Dr. James Dobson, *Dr. Dobson's Handbook of Family Advice* (Harvest House Publishers, 2012), 80.
2. Tony Merida, *Exalting Jesus in 1 and 2 Kings* (Nashville, TN: B&H Publishing Group), 271.
3. Mike Nappa, *The Courage to Be Christian: Entering a Life of Spiritual Passion* (West Monroe, LA: Howard Publishing, Co., Inc., 2001), 3.
4. James C. Goodloe IV, quoted in Timothy George, "Justice Scalia on Funeral Sermons," *First Things*, February 22, 2016.

PERSONAL QUESTIONS

1. What do you learn about grace from how Elisha promised a victory to a wicked king like Joash?

   a. What do you learn about grace by reading Romans 3:9-18 followed by Ephesians 2:8-9?

   b. How should being a recipient of God's grace and mercy impact others who act like the people described in Romans 3:9-18? (See Ephesians 4:32.)

2. Joash's victories were impacted by his lack of devotion (only striking the arrows three times). How is that a good illustration of the degree of victory we have in the Christian life? (See verses like Luke 11:9-13; James 4:2.)

   a. In what areas of your Christian life is your devotion the most consistent?

   b. In what areas could your devotion go to a deeper level?

   c. How do we keep from being more devoted without striving to please God with our works? How do we find the proper balance?

3. After you leave this earth, what part of your present life will still have an impact on others? (fruit that remains—John 15:5, 16)

   a. How is your spiritual life better as a result of prior generations who impacted you?

   b. What specific investments are you making now (time, talent, treasure), and in whom, will that continue as sources of light and life after you are gone?

GROUP QUESTIONS

1. Ask members to share their ideas about the modern notion of retirement.

   a. What is society's normal way of defining and applying the notion of retirement?

   b. For a Christian, what might be an alternative way(s) of defining retirement?

   c. What does a verse like Job 5:26 suggest about maturing and expanding one's life right up to the end? (Grain is harvested at the height of its ____________________.) In what ways did Elisha illustrate this idea?

2. Think about the idea of deliverance. From what has God delivered you?

a. What things would you like to experience deliverance from in the future?

b. What is the most important deliverance every Christian experiences? Deliverance from the ____________________and the__________________ of sin through Christ's death on the cross.

3. Colossians 3:23 talks about doing everything "heartily, as to the Lord." What does "heartily" mean?

   a. What does "as to the Lord" mean? Would we do the same task differently depending on whether Jesus or another person asked us?

b. How would we act differently if Jesus was our vocational boss, if we were married to Jesus, if we were raising Jesus as our child? Should we act differently?

4. How does our view of our destiny influence the devotion with which we approach our life?

DID YOU KNOW?

Several curious things happen in Elisha's exchange with Joash (2 Kings 13:14-19). First, Elisha tells Joash to shoot an arrow out "the east window." Why? Because the city of Aphek, where Joash would destroy the Syrians, was east of Samaria, in the Trans-Jordan. So Joash shot the arrow in the direction of his intended victory. Second, Elisha placed his hand on Joash's hand on the bow. Why? It was a type of "laying on of hands," a signal of the blessing of God from the prophet on Joash's endeavor. Joash had inherited a meager military force from his father, Jehoahaz, yet Elisha wasn't concerned. Why? He had seen innumerable chariots and horses from heaven (2 Kings 6:8-17) that Joash knew nothing of that could ensure a victory for Israel.

ADDITIONAL RESOURCES

by Dr. David Jeremiah

A LIFE BEYOND AMAZING

Love, joy, peace, endurance, humility—these are the traits Christ exhibited continually while on earth. Christ left us His Spirit after He ascended to heaven so that we might display these traits—"the fruit of the Spirit"—as well. In *A Life Beyond Amazing: 9 Decisions That Will Transform Your Life Today*, Dr. David Jeremiah explores the nine traits of the Spirit-filled life and explains that we can live an extraordinary life here on earth if we abide in Christ.

FORWARD

Many of us want our life to make a difference, but we aren't sure how to go about accomplishing that goal. Too often, life's circumstances can weigh us down and prevent us from living the life we desire. In *Forward* Dr. Jeremiah will take you through Scripture and teach you how to discover God's purpose for your life and then to move forward in it. God has a plan for your life!

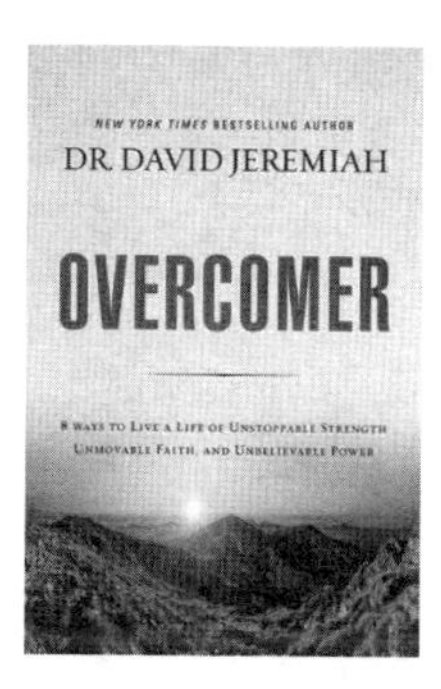

OVERCOMER

The idea of "overcoming" has transformed over time. When Christ came, the battlefield changed from plains and fields to the human mind and heart. In the *Overcomer* book, Dr. Jeremiah uses Paul's description of spiritual armor to teach us how we are called to overcome in this world of sin, explaining how, when we "put on" Christ, we can stand firm against the evil one.

SLAYING THE GIANTS

There's a breed of giants lurking in the shadows, keeping Christians from standing on the promises that accompany their salvation. Who are these giants? Look in our churches and you'll notice fear, discouragement, loneliness, worry, temptation, and guilt. In *Slaying the Giants*, Dr. David Jeremiah will help you discover how to recognize and banish these giants from your life!

Each of these resources was created from a teaching series by Dr. David Jeremiah. Contact Turning Point for more information about correlating materials.

For pricing information and ordering, contact us at

P.O. Box 3838
San Diego, CA 92163
(800) 947-1993
www.DavidJeremiah.org

STAY CONNECTED
to Dr. David Jeremiah

Take advantage of two great ways to let Dr. David Jeremiah give you spiritual direction every day!

Turning Points Magazine and Devotional

Receive Dr. David Jeremiah's magazine, *Turning Points*, each month:

- Thematic study focus
- 52 pages of life-changing reading
- Relevant articles
- Special features
- Daily devotional readings
- Bible study resource offers
- Live event schedule
- Radio & television information

Request *Turning Points* magazine today!

(800) 947-1993
www.DavidJeremiah.org/Magazine

Daily Turning Point E-Devotional

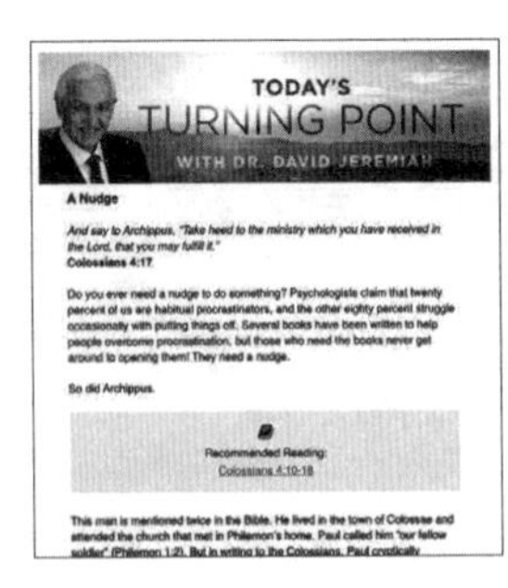

A Nudge

And say to Archippus, "Take heed to the ministry which you have received in the Lord, that you may fulfill it."
Colossians 4:17

Do you ever need a nudge to do something? Psychologists claim that twenty percent of us are habitual procrastinators, and the other eighty percent struggle occasionally with putting things off. Several books have been written to help people overcome procrastination, but those who need the books never get around to opening them! They need a nudge.

So did Archippus.

Recommended Reading:
Colossians 4:10-18

This man is mentioned twice in the Bible. He lived in the town of Colossae and attended the church that met in Philemon's home. Paul called him "our fellow soldier" (Philemon 1:2). But in writing to the Colossians, Paul cryptically

Start your day off right! Find words of inspiration and spiritual motivation waiting for you on your computer every morning! Receive a daily e-devotion communication from David Jeremiah that will strengthen your walk with God and encourage you to live the authentic Christian life.

Request your free e-devotional today!

(800) 947-1993
www.DavidJeremiah.org/Devo